# Adam Smith and the Death of David Hume

# Adam Smith and the Death of David Hume

## The *Letter to Strahan* and Related Texts

Edited by Dennis C. Rasmussen

LEXINGTON BOOKS/FORTRESS ACADEMIC
*Lanham • Boulder • New York • London*

Published by Lexington Books/Fortress Academic

Lexington Books is an imprint of The Rowman & Littlefield Publishing Group, Inc.
4501 Forbes Boulevard, Suite 200, Lanham, Maryland 20706
www.rowman.com

Unit A, Whitacre Mews, 26-34 Stannary Street, London SE11 4AB



British Library Cataloguing in Publication Information Available

**Library of Congress Cataloging-in-Publication Data Available**

ISBN 978-1-4985-8610-8 (cloth : alk. paper)
ISBN 978-1-4985-8611-5 (electronic)

∞™ The paper used in this publication meets the minimum requirements of American National Standard for Information Sciences—Permanence of Paper for Printed Library Materials, ANSI/NISO Z39.48-1992.

Printed in the United States of America

# Contents

# Acknowledgments

I would like to thank Jana Hodges-Kluck and Lexington Books for taking on this somewhat unusual project, as well as Sam Fleischacker for his many helpful suggestions. I am also grateful for the assistance provided by the staffs of the Tisch Library at Tufts University, the Widener and Lamont Libraries at Harvard University, the Beinecke Library at Yale University, the Morgan Library and Museum in New York, the British Library and Dr. Williams's Library in London, the Edinburgh University Library and the National Library of Scotland in Edinburgh, the University of Glasgow Library, and the Public Record Office of Northern Ireland in Belfast. Finally, I thank Princeton University Press for permission to reprint material from my book, *The Infidel and the Professor: David Hume, Adam Smith, and the Friendship That Shaped Modern Thought* (2017), in the introduction to this volume.

# Abbreviations

CAS *Correspondence of Adam Smith*, edited by Ernest Campbell Mossner and Ian Simpson Ross. Indianapolis: Liberty Fund, 1987.

HL *The Letters of David Hume*, edited by J. Y. T. Greig. Two volumes. Oxford: Clarendon, 1932.

NHL *New Letters of David Hume*, edited by Raymond Klibansky and Ernest C. Mossner. Oxford: Clarendon, 1954.

# Introduction

Adam Smith published three works under his name during his lifetime: *The Theory of Moral Sentiments* (1759), *An Inquiry into the Nature and Causes of the Wealth of Nations* (1776), and an ostensible letter on the last days, death, and character of David Hume, published as *Letter from Adam Smith, LL.D. to William Strahan, Esq.* (1777).[1] The first two are now extremely well known and the subject of an extensive and ever-growing scholarly literature, but the third much less so. The relative obscurity of the *Letter to Strahan* owes partly to the fact that it is a short, occasional piece rather than a full-length treatise. Yet in the eighteenth century it elicited almost as much commentary as did Smith's books, and its publication reveals much about both Smith's outlook and his character. The neglect of this work is also partly a result of the vagaries of modern scholarship, above all the fact that the version of the *Letter to Strahan* included in the standard (and generally excellent) *Glasgow Edition of the Works and Correspondence of Adam Smith* is decidedly wanting in certain crucial respects.[2] First, it is simply incorporated into the volume of Smith's correspondence, as if it were a private letter to his publisher rather than a work carefully crafted for publication; second, it contains several (albeit

1. Smith also published three short works—a preface to a collection of poems by William Hamilton (1748) and two letters to the *Edinburgh Review* (1755 and 1756)—anonymously, and he allowed some of his essays to be published posthumously as *Essays on Philosophical Subjects* (1795). His lecture notes and private correspondence were, of course, never intended to be published at all, at least in the form that we have them.

2. See CAS, 217–21.

fairly minor) typographical and transcription errors; and third, it contains no editorial apparatus to explain Smith's references. The present edition is designed to remedy these shortcomings, and to bring greater attention to this underappreciated work.

This introduction will discuss the context in which the *Letter to Strahan* was written; the composition, publication, and significance of the work; and the strong reaction that it provoked. Along the way it will also explain the relevance of the six supplementary texts that are included in this volume: David Hume's *My Own Life*, the work to which the *Letter to Strahan* was a kind of companion piece; two personal letters, one that is mentioned in the *Letter* and another that prefigures an important passage in it; and three published responses to the *Letter*—two viciously critical and one generally favorable.

## CONTEXT

Smith's closest friend for most of his adult life was David Hume—philosopher, historian, and notorious religious skeptic.[3] Nearly everything that Hume wrote touched on the topic of religion in one way or another: the credibility of the arguments in its favor, its psychological origins and consequences, its history, its effects on morality and politics. Though he never denied outright the existence of a higher power, he deemed the principal arguments on behalf of one to be highly implausible, and he considered the effects of religion to be mostly pernicious. As one scholar has written, "Hume's critique of religion and religious belief is . . . subtle, profound, and damaging to religion in ways that have no philosophical antecedents and few successors."[4] Hume sometimes presented his arguments in an artful or oblique manner—by attributing them to a character in a dialogue, for instance, or by clothing skeptical conclusions in the garb

---

3. For a book-length examination of Hume and Smith's friendship, see Dennis C. Rasmussen, *The Infidel and the Professor: David Hume, Adam Smith, and the Friendship That Shaped Modern Thought* (Princeton: Princeton University Press, 2017). The present introduction draws extensively on chapters 10–12 of this work, and I am grateful to Princeton University Press for permission to reuse this material.

4. J. C. A. Gaskin, "Hume on Religion," in *The Cambridge Companion to Hume*, second edition, ed. David Fate Norton and Jacqueline Taylor (Cambridge: Cambridge University Press, 2009), 480.

of fideistic wonder at the mysteries of God's ways—but the smokescreens were usually fairly transparent. His contemporaries were not fooled, nor did he particularly mean them to be. On the contrary, Hume often delighted in the prospect of eliciting "a murmur among the zealots."[5] As might be expected, he thereby earned a reputation for impiety: Hume was christened "the Great Infidel" and experienced a lifetime of abuse and reproach from the devout, including a concerted (though unsuccessful) effort to excommunicate him from the Church of Scotland in the mid-1750s.

When Hume fell seriously ill in 1776, his death became a highly anticipated event. As one bemused contemporary put it, during his final months "his situation became the universal topick of conversation and enquiry; each individual expressing an anxious solicitude about his health, as if he had been his intimate and particular friend."[6] The reason for this widespread interest, of course, was that everyone wanted to know how the notorious infidel would face his end. Would he show remorse or perhaps even recant his skepticism? Would he die in a state of distress, having none of the usual consolations afforded by belief in an afterlife? The *Monthly Review* captured the fixation nicely: "When men of such PARTS, and such PRINCIPLES, as those which distinguished the character and writings of Mr. Hume, come to face the immediate terrors of death, the world is always curious to learn in what manner they support the trying conflict: whether the near approach of that awful change of situation which they are about to experience, (in an hour wherein one would think, the boldest mortal would not dare either to DISSEMBLE or to TRIFLE) has produced any change in their *minds*; whether they continue fixed, and steady to their past professions; or, whether '*new light*' is let into 'the soul's dark cottage,' as the poet [Edmund Waller] expresses it, 'through the chinks' of its ruins,—opening wider, at the moment when the batter'd fabric is tottering to its dissolution."[7]

Hume was well aware of the intense curiosity that surrounded his looming death, and he was determined to die as he thought a philosopher should—cheerfully and tranquilly, without undue hopes or fears—and

5. See p. 37 in this volume.

6. [Samuel Jackson Pratt,] *Supplement to the Life of David Hume, Esq., Containing Genuine Anecdotes, and a Circumstantial Account of His Death and Funeral* (London: J. Bew, 1777), 40–41.

7. See the review of *The Life of David Hume, Esq.* in *The Monthly Review, or, Literary Journal*, vol. 56 (March 1777), 206.

to do it for a public audience. As part of this effort, in mid-April 1776 he wrote a brief autobiography, titled *My Own Life*, which is included in this volume.[8] Throughout the narrative he highlights his steady rise in the world, from relative obscurity to worldwide renown and from a slender patrimony to unexpected affluence. He also makes much of the poor reception of his publications, along with the optimistic and resilient temperament that enabled him to recover quickly from the disappointment each time. Yet he says surprisingly little—almost nothing, in fact—about the *contents* of his writings. A reader coming to *My Own Life* with no prior knowledge of Hume or his books would scarcely realize that she was reading the autobiography of a notorious infidel.[9] Of course, there was little need for Hume to dilate on his lack of piety: every reader of *My Own Life* would have been keenly aware of it. Indeed, Hume knew that many would scour the work for incriminating evidence—for some kind of sign that deep down he was depraved or despondent, fearful or remorseful. He was determined to frustrate these efforts, and indeed to demonstrate that the contrary was true.

The last two paragraphs drive the point home. In the penultimate paragraph Hume describes his state of mind in the face of a disease that he knew was "mortal and incurable." He observes that he now expects "a speedy dissolution" but that he has "never suffered a moment's abatement of my spirits . . . I possess the same ardour as ever in study, and the same gaiety in company."[10] The approach of death, in other words, did nothing to change his attitude, his views, or his lifestyle. He concludes the essay with an assessment of his own character that is written in the past tense, almost as if from beyond the grave. "I am, or rather was," he writes, "a man of mild dispositions, of command of temper, of an open, social, and cheerful humour, capable of attachment, but little susceptible of enmity, and of great moderation in all my passions. Even my love of literary

8. See pp. 35–43.

9. The only hints in the narrative to this effect are Hume's lament that the *Treatise* did not even manage to "excite a murmur among the zealots," his acknowledgment that he had "wantonly exposed" himself "to the rage of both civil and religious factions," and a pair of references to the aspersions cast on him by William Warburton and Richard Hurd: see pp. 37, 43, 38, and 40 in this volume, respectively. Even these hints are in a way counterbalanced by Hume's remark that the Archbishops of Canterbury and Armagh "separately sent me messages not to be discouraged" after the first volume of *The History of England* fared so poorly with the public: see p. 40 in this volume.

10. See pp. 42–43 in this volume.

fame, my ruling passion, never soured my temper, notwithstanding my frequent disappointments."[11] Though Hume *was* famously affable—he was a favorite among the Edinburgh literati, even the ministers, and the high society of Paris bestowed on him the honorific *le bon David*—this somewhat rose-colored self-portrait would be called into question by his critics.[12] Hume's intentions, though, are clear: he was trying not only to present his own character in a positive light but also to show that a skeptic could live and die with composure and grace.

A few days after completing *My Own Life*, Hume set out from his home in Edinburgh to consult the doctors in London about his health. Around the same time, Smith, not knowing of Hume's plans, headed north from London toward Edinburgh in order to see him. A lucky stroke prevented them from passing each other by: while Hume was resting at an inn in Morpeth, on the road between the two capitals, his valet happened to be standing at the gate when the carriage bearing Smith drew up.[13] This meeting marked the first time in three years that Hume and Smith were together in person. They soon parted ways once again, however, as Smith was obliged to proceed on to Scotland to see his mother, who was also ill and expected her son to arrive any day. Soon after arriving in London on May 1, Hume wrote to Smith to let him know that his health had improved somewhat and to apprise him of an important item that he had apparently forgotten to mention in Morpeth: "You will find among my Papers a very inoffensive Piece, called *My Own Life*," he writes, and "there can be no Objection, that this small piece shoud be sent to Messrs. Strahan and Cadell and the Proprietors of my other Works to be prefixed to any future Edition of them."[14]

On the advice of the doctors Hume soon moved on to Bath to take the waters there. His first trial of the waters appeared to be successful, but the good news did not last. Hume's health continued to deteriorate, and

11. See p. 43 in this volume.

12. See, for instance, footnote k on p. 67 in this volume.

13. See p. 45 in this volume.

14. David Hume to Adam Smith, 3 May 1776, in HL II, 318, and CAS, 196. Smith was, at this point, Hume's literary executor, while William Strahan (1715–1785) and Thomas Cadell (1742–1802) were Hume's (and Smith's) publishers. Hume's description of *My Own Life* as "very inoffensive" is clearly meant to distance it from his other posthumous publication, the controversial *Dialogues Concerning Natural Religion*, which will be discussed in the next section of this introduction.

toward the end of June he headed back to Scotland, finally arriving in Edinburgh on July 3. Though Hume and Smith had seen each other very little in the previous three years, they did their best to make up for lost time: Smith stayed at Hume's house in the New Town for most of the period from Hume's return to Edinburgh through mid-August.[15]

Alas, there is little surviving evidence of what they did or said during this time.[16] The only conversation between the two for which we have a detailed record took place on August 8. Smith first recounted the exchange in a letter to his friend Alexander Wedderburn, which is included in this volume, and then included a slightly different version in the *Letter to Strahan*.[17] The crux of the conversation revolved around Hume comparing his own situation to that of the characters in a dialogue by Lucian that he had recently reread. The characters were pleading with Charon—the boatman of Greek mythology who carried the souls of the recently deceased across the River Styx into Hades—in hopes of procuring a stay of execution. One hoped to first marry off a daughter, another to finish building his house, and a third to make some provisions for his young children. Hume tried to conjure up a similar excuse for himself, but he found that, having done almost everything that he had ever intended to do, he was unable to come up with any plausible candidates. In the version of the conversation that Smith related to Wedderburn, Hume then hits upon a possibility: "at last I thought I might say, Good Charon, I have been endeavouring to open the eyes of the people; have a little patience only till I have the pleasure of seeing the churches shut up, and the Clergy sent about their business."[18] In the *Letter to Strahan*, however, Smith softens Hume's barb somewhat, having him say: "Have a little patience, good Charon, I have been en-

15. See David Hume to John Home of Ninewells, 25 July 1776, in Sadao Ikeda, *David Hume and the Eighteenth Century British Thought: An Annotated Catalogue* (Tokyo: Chuo University Library, 1986), 219.

16. We do have one fleeting reference in a letter that Hume wrote on July 16. The weather was magnificent, but Hume was unable to venture out of the house to enjoy it, and he writes that "instead of grudging that I cannot partake, directly, of this Pleasure; Mr Smith tells me, that I ought to enjoy it by Sympathy, which I endeavour to do." David Hume to John Home, 16 July 1776, in Gerhard Streminger, "David Hume and John Home: Two New Letters," *Hume Studies* 10.1 (April 1984), 81.

17. See pp. 55–56 and 47–48 in this volume, respectively. Alexander Wedderburn, 1st Earl of Rosslyn (1733–1805), was at this time a Member of Parliament and the solicitor general, and he would later become Britain's Lord Chancellor. In 1755–1756 he was also the principal editor of both issues of the short-lived *Edinburgh Review*, to which Smith was a contributor.

18. See p. 56 in this volume.

deavouring to open the eyes of the Public. If I live a few years longer, I may have the satisfaction of seeing the downfal of some of the prevailing systems of superstition."[19] As we will see, this passage—even toned down as it was—ended up becoming one of the two most commented-upon elements of the *Letter*.

A day or two after this conversation—it is unclear exactly when—Smith departed for his home in Kirkcaldy, finding that Hume was so weak that "even my company fatigues him, especially as his spirits are so good that he cannot help talking incessantly when anybody is with him."[20] In his final letter to Hume, written on August 22, Smith presented him with a proposition: "If you will give me leave I will add a few lines to your account of your own life; giving some account, in my own name, of your behaviour in this illness, if, contrary to my own hopes, it should prove your last."[21] In other words, Smith was requesting permission to complete his friend's autobiography, in a sense, bringing the narrative of *My Own Life* from April 18, where the work leaves off, up to Hume's death. Knowing the keen public interest in how Hume approached his end, Smith wanted to write the "authorized" version of the story, and to demonstrate to the world that Hume had died as a philosopher should. Smith provides Hume a hint of what the work would look like: "Some conversations we had lately together," he writes, "particularly that concerning your want of an excuse to make to Charon, the excuse you at last thought of, and the very bad reception which Charon was likely to give it, would, I imagine, make no disagreeable part of the history." While Smith would later express surprise that the *Letter to Strahan* provoked so much outrage, then, in fact he knew—or should have known—from the very beginning that it would do so: this conversation was hardly calculated to soothe the sensibilities of the pious. Smith also planned to emphasize Hume's continual good spirits in the face of a protracted and obviously fatal illness: "You have in a declining state of health, under an exhausting disease, for more than two years together, now looked at the approach, or what you at least believed to be the approach of Death with a steady chearfulness such as very few men have been able to maintain for a few hours, tho'

19. See p. 48 in this volume.
20. See p. 56 in this volume.
21. Adam Smith to David Hume, 22 August 1776, in CAS, 206.

otherwise in the most perfect Health."[22] This, clearly, was a story that the public needed to hear.

Hume received Smith's letter the next day, and his reply was the last letter he ever wrote. By this point he was so weak that he was forced to dictate the note to his nephew, rather than penning it himself. "I go very fast to decline," Hume tells Smith, although not quite fast enough for his tastes: "last night [I] had a small fever, which I hoped might put a quicker period to this tedious Illness, but unluckily it has in a great measure gone off." He also gives Smith complete discretion to complete his autobiography in whatever way he deems suitable: "You are too good in thinking any trifles that concern me are so much worth your attention, but I give you entire liberty to make what Additions you please to the account of my Life."[23] While Hume's tone here is cheerfully complaisant, this was no small proposition that he was accepting. *My Own Life* was, after all, Hume's final message to his readers, the one that would serve as the preface to future editions of his collected works. His immediate willingness to grant Smith "entire liberty" regarding such a central ingredient of his posthumous legacy reveals an extraordinary degree of trust and confidence. Hume died two days later, on August 25, at the age of sixty-five.

Given Hume's reputation for impiety, any comment on the manner of his death in the succeeding months was bound to attract attention. The "authorized" account of his last days by his best friend was sure to be the subject of intense scrutiny.

## INTERLUDE: THE *DIALOGUES* CONTROVERSY

*My Own Life* and Smith's supplement to it were not the only publications that Hume and Smith discussed during Hume's final months and days. Much of their correspondence during this period, in fact, was taken up with a running disagreement over the fate of Hume's *Dialogues Concerning Natural Religion*. When Hume drew up his will in January 1776 he named Smith his literary executor, and one of the duties that he sought to

22. Ibid.
23. David Hume to Adam Smith, 23 August 1776, in HL II, 336, and CAS, 208.

bestow upon his friend was that of overseeing the posthumous publication of the *Dialogues*.[24] But Smith resolutely refused to carry out this request. It is often claimed that this episode significantly tarnished their friendship and caused Hume great pain during his final months, and Smith's behavior is generally seen as unnecessarily cautious, utterly inexplicable, or even an act of betrayal—a denial of his best friend's dying wish.[25] It has even been suggested that it was Smith's residual feelings of guilt over this dispute that motivated him to write the *Letter to Strahan*; according to this view, Smith's eulogy was written "to salve his own conscience."[26] It will thus be helpful to briefly consider this episode in order to show that in all likelihood Smith felt no guilt over it, nor did he have any real reason to.[27]

To begin with, there is little evidence to support the common claim that the disagreement between Hume and Smith over the *Dialogues* was particularly acrimonious. Hume was clearly partial to the work and anxious to see it published, but the idea that Smith's refusal to take on this responsibility caused Hume great pain seems decidedly exaggerated. Indeed, Hume's feelings of affection toward Smith do not seem to have diminished in the slightest. The first letter that Hume wrote on the subject—in which he tells Smith that his scruples over the *Dialogues* are "groundless"—concludes with a characteristic plea for Smith to write more often, along with an equally characteristic expression of regret at not being together in person: "If you write to me, hem! hem! I say, if you write to me, send your Letters under Cover to Mr Strahan, who will have my Direction. I regret much, in leaving Edinburgh, that I shall lose much of your Company, which I shoud have enjoy'd this Summer."[28] Soon afterward, as we have seen, Hume invited Smith to stay at his house for

24. See HL II, 317 n. 1.

25. Such views are common even among scholars who are ordinarily highly sympathetic to Smith. See, for instance, Ryan Patrick Hanley, "Skepticism and Imagination: Smith's Response to Hume's *Dialogues*," in *New Essays on Adam Smith's Moral Philosophy*, ed. Wade L. Robison and David B. Suits (Rochester: Rochester Institute of Technology Press, 2012), 173; Gavin Kennedy, *Adam Smith's Lost Legacy* (New York: Palgrave Macmillan, 2005), 9–10; Nicholas Phillipson, *Adam Smith: An Enlightened Life* (New Haven: Yale University Press, 2010), 244, 242; and Ian Simpson Ross, *The Life of Adam Smith*, second edition (Oxford: Oxford University Press, 2010), 319, 359–60, 445.

26. Ernest Campbell Mossner, *The Life of David Hume*, second edition (Oxford: Clarendon, 1980), 605.

27. For a fuller examination of this episode, see Rasmussen, *The Infidel and the Professor*, chapter 10.

28. David Hume to Adam Smith, 3 May 1776, in HL II, 317, and CAS, 195.

over a month, from the time of his return to Edinburgh on July 3 through mid-August, just a couple of weeks before his death. In his final days, we have also seen, Hume immediately granted Smith complete discretion to "make what Additions you please" to *My Own Life*.[29] His last letter to Smith both opens and closes by calling him "My Dearest Friend."[30] None of this suggests a serious falling out or deep-seated feelings of resentment.

The main question confounding most scholars, though, is *why* Smith was so adamant in his refusal to publish the *Dialogues*. One surprisingly common answer to this question has been that Smith objected to the contents of the *Dialogues*—that he was disturbed or even scandalized by the work, or saw it as deeply incompatible with his own philosophy, or was personally unable to come to grips with Hume's barrage of skepticism.[31] This answer raises an extremely thorny question of its own, one that cannot be dealt with fully here, namely that of Smith's religious views. Smith generally went to great lengths, in both his writings and his personal life, to avoid revealing his religious beliefs (or perhaps lack thereof),[32] and as a result there is little consensus as to his views on this score. The conjectures range from sincere Christian belief to closet atheism, though the majority of scholars come down somewhere in the middle, reading Smith as a deist of some kind.[33] However one reads Smith's religious views more broadly,

29. David Hume to Adam Smith, 23 August 1776, in HL II, 36, and CAS, 208.

30. David Hume to Adam Smith, 23 August 1776, in HL II, 335–36, and CAS, 208.

31. See, for instance, T. D. Campbell and Ian Ross, "The Theory and Practice of the Wise and Virtuous Man: Reflections on Adam Smith's Response to Hume's Deathbed Wish," *Studies in Eighteenth-Century Culture* 11 (1982), 70–72; Karl Graf Ballestrem, "David Hume und Adam Smith: Zur philosophischen Dimension einer Freundschaft," in *Adam Smith als Moralphilosoph*, ed. Christel Fricke and Hans-Peter Schütt (Berlin: Walter de Gruyter, 2005), 344–45; Brendan Long, "Adam Smith's Theism," in *The Elgar Companion to Adam Smith*, ed. Jeffrey T. Young (Cheltenham, UK: Edward Elgar, 2009), 81–82; Annette C. Baier, *The Pursuits of Philosophy: An Introduction to the Life and Thought of David Hume* (Cambridge, MA: Harvard University Press, 2011), 121; and Hanley, "Skepticism and Imagination."

32. Contemporaries frequently noted that Smith was "very guarded in conversation" when the topic of religion came up. John Ramsay of Ochtertyre, *Scotland and Scotsmen in the Eighteenth Century*, ed. Alexander Allardyce, vol. 1 (Edinburgh: William Blackwood, 1888), 463; see also 467.

33. Among the works that go furthest in reading Smith as a *Christian* believer (as opposed to a deist) are Long, "Adam Smith's Theism," and several of the essays collected in Paul Oslington, ed., *Adam Smith as Theologian* (New York: Routledge, 2011). The most detailed reading of Smith as a closet atheist, at least later in his life, can be found in Peter Minowitz, *Profits, Priests, and Princes: Adam Smith's Emancipation of Economics from Politics and Religion* (Stanford: Stanford University Press, 1993), especially chapters 6–10.

the texts collected in this volume call very much into doubt the idea that he was overly disturbed by Hume's skepticism. In the *Letter to Strahan* he publicly describes Hume as a paragon of wisdom and virtue,[34] and in the letter to Wedderburn he comments that "poor David Hume is dying very fast, but with great chearfulness and good humour and with more real resignation to the necessary course of things, than any whining Christian ever dyed with pretended resignation to the will of God."[35] Nor is there any indication that these statements represented a last-minute change of heart, spurred by guilt over the *Dialogues* episode. Smith was, after all, best friends with Hume for more than a quarter of a century, and they frequently joked about religion in their letters to one another, with Smith's irony on the subject just as pronounced and transparent as Hume's. As Emma Rothschild rightly remarks, their correspondence reveals a sense of "intimacy and complicity" that seems "difficult to reconcile with the presumption of serious religious differences."[36]

This general reading of Smith's stance toward Hume and Hume's religious skepticism is corroborated by some of his statements and actions related to the *Dialogues* itself. During the course of his correspondence with Hume and William Strahan on the work, Smith promised time and again that he would be "very happy" to take "every possible measure" to ensure that the work would be "most carefully preserved," and he also deemed it "finely written"—he just wished that it "had remained in Manuscript to be communicated only to a few people."[37] In other words, while Smith seems to have thought that such bold criticisms of religion are best kept away from the public eye, he had no problem with the idea of circulating the work among friends. In fact, Smith appears to have actively disseminated the work himself—how widely we do not know—as we have a letter from

34. See p. 51 in this volume.

35. See p. 55 in this volume.

36. Emma Rothschild, *Economic Sentiments: Adam Smith, Condorcet, and the Enlightenment* (Cambridge, MA: Harvard University Press, 2001), 301 n. 84; see also 130. For an exchange between Rothschild and Samuel Fleischacker on this point, see Samuel Fleischacker, "Smith's Ambiguities: A Response to Emma Rothschild's *Economic Sentiments*," *Adam Smith Review* 1 (2004), 143–44; and Emma Rothschild, "Dignity or Meanness," *Adam Smith Review* 1 (2004), 160–61. Once again, this is a point that I seek to substantiate throughout *The Infidel and the Professor*.

37. Adam Smith to David Hume, 16 June 1776, in CAS, 201–2; Adam Smith to David Hume, 22 August 1776, in CAS, 206; Adam Smith to William Strahan, 5 September 1776, in CAS, 211.

the duc de La Rochefoucauld (the moralist's great-great-great-grandson) thanking Smith for sending a copy of the *Dialogues* to him in France almost immediately after it was released.[38]

The likeliest explanation for Smith's refusal to publish the *Dialogues* is also the simplest. As he himself indicated in a pair of draft letters that he wrote (but never actually sent) to Strahan, he was wary of the public "clamour" that the book would provoke and the effects that this clamor would have on his own "quiet" and on Hume's posthumous reputation.[39] Was this, then, an instance of excessive caution, or even cowardice—something about which Smith should feel guilty—as is often suggested? If it was, then it was a failing that was not unique to Smith: every one of Hume's friends who knew about the *Dialogues* urged him not to publish it, at least if the surviving record is anything to go by. We know that Gilbert Elliot opposed publication, as we have a letter from Hume to Elliot in which he complains: "Is it not hard & tyrannical in you, more tyrannical than any Act of the Stuarts, not to allow me to publish my Dialogues? Pray, do you not think that a proper Dedication may atone for what is exceptional in them?"[40] Hugh Blair likewise admonished Hume, "for Gods sake let that be a posthumous work, if ever it shall see the light: Tho' I really think it had better not."[41] We have a report that Adam Ferguson too "remonstrated" against publishing the work.[42] And Strahan, who was

38. See the duc de La Rochefoucauld to Adam Smith, 6 August 1779, in CAS, 238.

39. Adam Smith to William Strahan, October 1776, in CAS, 216; and Adam Smith to William Strahan, October 1776, in CAS, 216–17.

40. David Hume to Gilbert Elliot of Minto, 12 March 1763, in NHL, 71. Sir Gilbert Elliot, 3rd Baronet of Minto (1722–1777), was a Member of Parliament and an influential literary patron. He and Hume had been close friends since they were students together at Edinburgh University, and Hume consulted Elliot not just on the publication of the *Dialogues* but also on the content: see David Hume to Gilbert Elliot of Minto, 10 March 1751, in HL I, 153–56.

41. Hugh Blair to David Hume, 29 September 1763, in NHL, 73 n. 4. Blair (1718–1800) was a longtime chair of rhetoric and belles lettres at Edinburgh University and minister of the biggest and most prestigious church in Scotland, St. Giles' Cathedral. He was a close friend of Hume's; among other things, he helped to prevent Hume's excommunication from the Church of Scotland in the mid-1750s and rented Hume's apartment in the Lawnmarket during the latter's travels in France.

42. Anne Keith to Sir Robert Murray Keith, 6 November 1776, Public Record Office of Northern Ireland, D2433/D/1/25. Ferguson (1723–1816) was an important philosopher and historian in his own right; his best-known work is *An Essay on the History of Civil Society* (1767). In 1762 he was a prime mover in the founding of the Poker Club, a group of which Hume and Smith were both also original members. Hume and Ferguson did not always see eye to eye philosophically, but their personal relations were generally extremely cordial.

close to Hume personally as well as professionally, ultimately declined to publish the *Dialogues*—and this after he had, unlike Smith, promised Hume that he would do so.[43]

If the unanimous counsel of some of Hume's closest friends is not enough to exonerate Smith from charges of cowardice, then Hume's own words and actions should be. Despite Hume's greater willingness to court controversy and despite his obvious fondness for the *Dialogues*, he himself had refrained from publishing the work for *two and a half decades*.[44] Indeed, he did not even mention the manuscript's existence to his publisher until just a couple of months before his death.[45] He did ponder the possibility of publication from time to time, as the letter to Elliot quoted above suggests, but he realized that it would be an audacious move, even for him—hence his acknowledgment, in that letter, that there is something "exceptionable" about the work that would require a proper dedication to "atone for." Even more striking is Hume's explanation, in a letter to Strahan of June 1776 asking him to take on responsibility for the *Dialogues*, of why he had not published long ago: "I have hitherto forborne to publish it, because I was of late desirous to live quietly, and keep remote from all Clamour: For though it be not more exceptionable than some things I had formerly published; yet you know some of these were thought very exceptionable; and in prudence, perhaps, I ought to have suppressed them. I there introduce a Sceptic [i.e., the character Philo], who is indeed refuted, and at last gives up the Argument . . . yet before he is silenced, he advances several Topics, which will give Umbrage, and will be deemed very bold and free."[46] In other words, up until his final illness Hume had refrained from publishing the *Dialogues* for the exact same reason that Smith refused to do so: because it would create a "clamor" that would prevent him from living "quietly." Even the wording of their explanations is nearly identical.

---

43. See William Strahan to John Home of Ninewells, 3 March 1777, in *Letters of David Hume to William Strahan*, ed. G. Birkbeck Hill (Oxford: Clarendon, 1888), 362 n. 1.

44. Hume wrote the first draft of the *Dialogues* in the early 1750s. He returned to the work several times in subsequent years, revising it just after *The Natural History of Religion* appeared in print in 1757, making some more changes in the early 1760s, and finally adding a few polishing touches in 1776. See M. A. Stewart, "The Dating of Hume's Manuscripts," in *The Scottish Enlightenment: Essays in Reinterpretation*, ed. Paul Wood (Rochester: University of Rochester Press, 2000), especially 291, 300–303.

45. See David Hume to William Strahan, 8 June 1776, in HL II, 323–24.

46. Ibid.

The more perplexing question, in a way, is not why Smith refused to publish the *Dialogues* but rather why Hume was suddenly so adamant about publication after holding the work back for twenty-five years, and even more why he sought to foist this obligation on Smith. Hume may have reckoned that he had little left to lose at that point, with one foot almost in the grave, but obviously Smith was not in the same position. Moreover, Hume knew full well that Smith was always anxious to preserve his privacy and tranquility—his "quiet." It would not have taken a great feat of sympathy to realize that Smith would be averse to the public "clamor" that Hume himself foresaw would be provoked by the *Dialogues*. Nor should it be forgotten that Hume asked Smith to bear this burden so soon after *The Wealth of Nations* was published, on March 9, 1776. Given the many years of painstaking effort that Smith had poured into the book, the great anticipation that surrounded its release, and Smith's high hopes that its arguments would prove influential in both thought and practice, this was among the worst possible times for him to become mired in public controversy. (As we will see, this context made the *Letter to Strahan* all the more daring.) All things considered, then, Hume's part in this exchange is more difficult to account for than Smith's.

## COMPOSITION

Smith composed his supplement to Hume's *My Own Life* in the form of an ostensible letter to William Strahan, who was a Scot based in London and a dominant figure in the book industry; he had published a number of Hume's works as well as Smith's *The Wealth of Nations*. He also became Hume's literary executor after Smith refused to see the *Dialogues* through the press.[47] The *Letter* was addressed to Strahan because he was the person responsible for publishing *My Own Life* and thus also Smith's addition to it.[48] Smith opens the work by describing it as an "account of the behaviour of our late excellent friend, Mr. Hume, during his last illness."[49] His nar-

47. For the August 7 codicil to Hume's will, see HL II, 453.

48. Smith wrote to Hume's brother, "I think there is a propriety in addressing it as a letter to Mr Strahan to whom he [Hume] has left the care of his works." Adam Smith to John Home of Ninewells, 7 October 1776, in CAS, 214.

49. See p. 45 in this volume.

rative begins where *My Own Life* leaves off, in late April 1776. The first few pages are fairly straightforward: Smith describes Hume's decision to travel to London to consult the doctors there; their fortuitous encounter at Morpeth; the advice of the London doctors to visit Bath to take the waters; the temporary abeyance of Hume's illness at Bath, followed by the return of the symptoms "with their usual violence"; and Hume's return to his home and friends in Edinburgh. Back in Scotland, Smith notes, Hume's growing weakness did not prevent him from living as he always had: "he continued to divert himself, as usual, with correcting his own works for a new edition, with reading books of amusement, with the conversation of his friends; and, sometimes in the evening, with a party at his favourite game of whist."[50]

Smith then moves on to describe some of Hume's conversations with his doctors and friends in order to illustrate his cheerful mood during this period. He also mentions a touching letter that Hume's old friend James Edmonstoune of Newton wrote to him on August 7, bidding him a heartfelt goodbye. (The letter is included in this volume.[51]) The centerpiece of Smith's *Letter*, in many respects, is his recounting of the playful conversation that he and Hume had the following day about Charon. This conversation too served as a testament of Hume's composure and tranquility in the face of death, though Smith toned down, as we have seen, one of Hume's more stridently antireligious remarks.

Smith was no longer in Hume's company during his friend's last two weeks, having returned to Kirkcaldy in mid-August, so he carries the narrative forward through extracts from three letters. The extracts are taken from an August 22 report from Hume's physician, Joseph Black, on Hume's declining health and good spirits; Hume's last letter to Smith, written in his nephew's hand; and Black's announcement of Hume's death and account of his "happy composure of mind" in the moments leading up to it.[52] Presumably Smith wanted to include these letters as hard evidence of Hume's cheerfulness in his final days, so that the reader would not have to simply accept his word for it.[53]

---

50. See p. 46 in this volume.
51. See pp. 53–54.
52. See pp. 49–50 in this volume.
53. See Smith's comment to Strahan that he was striving to write "a very well authenticated account" of Hume's final illness: Adam Smith to William Strahan, 5 September 1776, in CAS, 211.

In the concluding paragraph Smith attempts to sum up Hume's character, confirming—even amplifying—Hume's self-presentation in *My Own Life*. As Smith's biographer Ian Simpson Ross rightly notes, this passage is "a beautifully flighted piece of prose, perhaps the best Smith ever wrote."[54] Smith opens with a preamble that must have been at least partly disingenuous: "Thus died our most excellent, and never to be forgotten friend; concerning whose philosophical opinions men will, no doubt, judge variously, every one approving or condemning them, according as they happen to coincide or disagree with his own; but concerning whose character and conduct there can scarce be a difference of opinion."[55] While Hume's affable demeanor did disarm a number of critics whom he met in person, Smith must have known that some—likely many—of his readers would disagree vociferously with the idea that a skeptic like Hume could have been of unimpeachable character. Even so, he proceeds to make his case, describing Hume's balanced temper, frugality, charity, generosity, gentle nature, firm mind, steady resolutions, delicacy, modesty, gaiety, extensive learning, and depth of thought. Perhaps most of all, he emphasizes Hume's ready sense of humor, his talent for enjoyable conversation, and his exceptional capacity for friendship.

Smith concludes the *Letter* with one of the most fateful sentences that he ever wrote: "Upon the whole, I have always considered him, both in his lifetime and since his death, as approaching as nearly to the idea of a perfectly wise and virtuous man, as perhaps the nature of human frailty will permit."[56] This sentence would draw even more attention from critics than the badinage about Charon. Smith was clearly echoing Plato's epitaph for Socrates in the concluding sentence of the *Phaedo*, in which the narrator, Phaedo, pronounces Socrates to be "of all those whom we knew in our time, the bravest and also the wisest and most upright."[57] This association of his friend's end with one of the most iconic deaths in the Western tradition, while audacious, was not the aspect of the sentence that proved most controversial. The real scandal, rather, was Smith's assertion that Hume, an avowed skeptic, was a model of wisdom and virtue.

54. Ross, *The Life of Adam Smith*, 323.

55. See p. 50 in this volume.

56. See p. 51 in this volume.

57. Plato, *Phaedo*, in *The Collected Dialogues of Plato*, ed. Edith Hamilton and Huntington Cairns (Princeton: Princeton University Press, 1961), 98.

Smith seems to have begun writing the *Letter* in late September 1776.[58] He dated the work November 9, but he had finished a draft by October 7, at which point he asked for comments on it from Hume's physician, Joseph Black—presumably because two of his letters are, as we have seen, quoted in the work—and from Hume's brother.[59] Black, in turn, also solicited the thoughts of their mutual friend John Home, the playwright—who is also mentioned in the *Letter*[60]—and some other friends.[61] After making a few revisions, Smith sent the final version to Strahan on November 13.[62]

## PUBLICATION

Hume had instructed both Smith and Strahan that his autobiography should be "prefixed to any future Edition" of his works, and that is how Smith assumed *My Own Life* and the *Letter to Strahan* would be issued.[63] From the outset, however—even before he had seen either of the pieces—Strahan wanted to publish them separately, as well.[64] When Strahan received Smith's letter he liked it "exceedingly," but he found that it was too short, even when paired with *My Own Life*, to "make a Volume even of the *smallest Size*." He proposed to combine them with some letters on political subjects that

58. In a draft letter to Strahan, probably written in late October 1776, Smith comments that when he had received Strahan's letter of 16 September "I had not begun the small addition which I proposed to make to the life of our late friend. It is now more than three weeks since I finished it." Adam Smith to William Strahan, October 1776, in CAS, 216.

59. See ibid.; and Adam Smith to John Home of Ninewells, 7 October 1776, in CAS, 214. Hume's brother responded: "I much approve of your thought in addressing it in a letter to Mr Strahan; as well as of the whole performance, only you will forgive me, for observeing that as it is to be aded, to what is wrote in so short and simple a manner would have wished, that the detail had been less minutely entered into, particularly of the journey, which being of a private concern, and haveing drawn to no consequences, does not interest the publick. But on the other hand, when I consider, that any alterations, might require the new modeling of the whole: as well as with what diffidence, I must give my oppinion when deviating from you I beleive it had best be published as it is." John Home of Ninewells to Adam Smith, 14 October 1776, in CAS, 214–15.

60. See p. 45 in this volume.

61. See Adam Smith to William Strahan, October 1776, in CAS, 216.

62. See Adam Smith to William Strahan, 13 November 1776, in CAS, 221.

63. David Hume to Adam Smith, 3 May 1776, in HL II, 318, and CAS, 196; see also David Hume to William Strahan, 8 June 1776, in HL II, 323; and Adam Smith to William Strahan, 5 September 1776, in CAS, 211.

64. See William Strahan to Adam Smith, 16 September 1776, in CAS, 212.

Hume had written to him over the years and asked for Smith's opinion on the matter, promising to "do nothing without your Advice and Approbation."[65] Smith quickly thwarted this idea. While "sensible that many of Mr Humes letters would do him great honour and that [Strahan] would publish none but such as would," Smith insisted that they ought to respect Hume's wishes above all else, and he had made it clear that he did not want any of his papers published beyond *My Own Life* and the *Dialogues*. "I know he always disliked the thought of his letters ever being published," Smith notes—ignoring for the moment the fact that he himself included Hume's last letter in his soon-to-be-published account of his friend's dying days.[66]

Smith did implicitly consent to the separate publication of *My Own Life* and the *Letter to Strahan*, however, commenting that they "will not make a volume; but [they] will make a small pamphlet."[67] That is accordingly how Strahan and his partner, Thomas Cadell, issued the two works in March 1777, under the title *The Life of David Hume, Esq., Written By Himself*—in order, they said, "to gratify the impatience of the public curiosity."[68] The first edition, published on March 11, consisted of 2,000 copies, and Strahan and Cadell printed another 1,000 copies in April.[69] Somewhat mysteriously, however, both *My Own Life* and the *Letter to Strahan* had already appeared in full in the January 1777 issue of the *Scots Magazine*.[70] It is unclear how this prepublication came about, or under

---

65. William Strahan to Adam Smith, 26 November 1776, in CAS, 222.

66. Adam Smith to William Strahan, 2 December 1776, in CAS, 223.

67. Adam Smith to William Strahan, 2 December 1776, in CAS, 224. Hume's brother was opposed to the idea of issuing the works in a separate pamphlet: see John Home of Ninewells to William Strahan, 25 February 1777, in Hill, *Letters of David Hume to William Strahan*, 361; and John Home of Ninewells to William Strahan, 13 March 1777, in Hill, *Letters of David Hume to William Strahan*, 363.

68. The full printer's note in *The Life of David Hume* reads as follows: "Mr. Hume, a few months before his death, wrote the following short account of his own Life; and, in a codicil to his will, desired that it might be prefixed to the next edition of his Works. That edition cannot be published for a considerable time. The Editor, in the mean while, in order to serve the purchasers of the former editions; and, at the same time, to gratify the impatience of the public curiosity; has thought proper to publish it separately, without altering even the title or superscription, which was written in Mr. Hume's own hand on the cover of the manuscript." *The Life of David Hume, Esq., Written By Himself* (London: Printed for W. Strahan; and T. Cadell, in the Strand, 1777), iii–iv.

69. See William B. Todd, "David Hume: A Preliminary Bibliography," in *Hume and the Enlightenment: Essays Presented to Ernest Campbell Mossner*, ed. William B. Todd (Edinburgh: Edinburgh University Press, 1974), 202–3.

70. See *Scots Magazine*, vol. 39 (January 1777), 1–7.

whose auspices; the correspondence of the relevant parties is entirely silent on the matter, as if it never happened.[71] In any case, the separate publication of *My Own Life* and the *Letter to Strahan* so soon after Hume's death—much earlier than they would have appeared had Strahan waited to include them in the next edition of Hume's collected works, per Hume's instructions—conferred on these pieces a prominence that they would not otherwise have had.

In addition to the 3,000 copies of *The Life of David Hume* issued by Strahan and Cadell and the printing of *My Own Life* and the *Letter to Strahan* in the *Scots Magazine*, the two were also published in full in the *Weekly Magazine, or Edinburgh Amusement* in March 1777; as a pamphlet in Dublin in 1777 and in Philadelphia in 1778; and in a French translation by Jean-Baptiste-Antoine Suard in 1777.[72] The *Letter to Strahan* was also published in full on its own, without *My Own Life* to accompany it, in the *Westminster Magazine* in April 1777, and almost in full in the *Monthly Review, or, Literary Journal* in March 1777.[73] In all, then, it was not long before there were more than enough copies of these works in circulation to satisfy the public curiosity—and provoke the pious.

## SIGNIFICANCE

*My Own Life* has received a good deal of scholarly attention, but the *Letter to Strahan* has not.[74] As we will see in the next section, things were

71. See Iain Gordon Brown, "Introduction: 'Embalming a Philosopher'—The Writing, Reception, and Resonance of David Hume's 'My Own Life,'" in *David Hume: My Own Life*, ed. Iain Gordon Brown (Edinburgh: Royal Society of Edinburgh, 2014), 23–24.

72. See *The Weekly Magazine, or Edinburgh Amusement*, vol. 35 (13 March 1777), 353–57; *The Weekly Magazine, or Edinburgh Amusement*, vol. 35 (20 March 1777), 388–91; *The Life of David Hume, Esq. Written By Himself, To Which is Added, A Letter from Adam Smith, LL.D. to William Strahan, Esq.* (Dublin: Printed for J. Williams, 1777); *The Life of David Hume, Esq; The Philosopher and Historian, Written By Himself* (Philadelphia: Printed and sold by Robert Bell, 1778); and *La vie de David Hume, écrite par lui-même: Traduite de l'Anglois* (Londres, 1777).

73. See "ACCOUNT of the DEATH of DAVID HUME, Esq. in a LETTER from ADAM SMITH, LL.D. to WILLIAM STRAHAN, Esq." *Westminster Magazine*, vol. 5 (April 1777), 211–13; and "Art. X. *The Life of David Hume, Esq*; Written by himself. 8vo. 1s. 6d. Cadell. 1777," *The Monthly Review, or, Literary Journal*, vol. 56 (March 1777), 210–13.

74. The more substantial scholarly discussions of the *Letter to Strahan* to date include Andrew Corsa, "Modern Greatness of Soul in Hume and Smith," *Ergo, an Open Access Jour-*

quite otherwise in the eighteenth century, when the *Letter to Strahan* caused a great uproar. It is one of the ambitions of this volume to inspire more scholars to explore the meanings and significance of the *Letter*. For the purposes of this introduction, however, a few general remarks on this score will suffice.

First, and most obviously, the *Letter* is a moving eulogy. As an early twentieth-century biographer of Hume, J. Y. T. Greig, writes, "No man could ask, and few have ever had, a finer tribute from a friend."[75] Even leaving aside the contents of the *Letter*, the very fact that Smith chose, of his own accord, to complete Hume's account of his life constitutes a remarkable compliment. If a friend is truly "another self," as Aristotle claimed, then Smith was undoubtedly the single best-placed person to round out Hume's autobiographical sketch.[76] And Smith's description of Hume's character and conduct is about as laudatory as it could be within the bounds of plausibility, not to say veracity.[77] Hume's irrepressible good spirits, unbroken equanimity, prodigious intellect, and engaging sense of humor are chronicled with an assurance and affection that only a close friend could bring to the narrative. It is evident that Smith considered himself lucky to have known someone of Hume's goodness and greatness so well, and for so long.

Somewhat less obviously, the *Letter to Strahan* also represents a kind of paean to friendship.[78] Smith opens the work by announcing his inten-

---

*nal of Philosophy* 2.2 (2015), especially 46–55; Chad Flanders, "Hume's Death and Smith's Philosophy," in *New Essays on Adam Smith's Moral Philosophy*, ed. Wade L. Robison and David B. Suits (Rochester: Rochester Institute of Technology Press, 2012), especially 195–200; Rasmussen, *The Infidel and the Professor*, chapter 12; and Eric Schliesser, "Obituary of a Vain Philosopher: Adam Smith's Reflections on Hume's Life," *Hume Studies* 29.2 (November 2003), 327–62.

75. J. Y. T. Greig, *David Hume* (New York: Garland, [1931] 1983), 414.

76. Aristotle, *Nicomachean Ethics*, trans. Robert C. Bartlett and Susan D. Collins (Chicago: University of Chicago Press, 2011), 194 and 203.

77. Smith's claim, in a draft letter to Strahan, that the *Letter* was written "without one word of flattery or compliment" is somewhat bewildering: see Adam Smith to William Strahan, October 1776, in CAS, 216. As for the veracity of Smith's description of Hume, Hume's biographer gave it a ringing endorsement: "In 1777 Adam Smith, who was closest to Hume in intellect and spirit, gave the world the most famous portrait of *le bon David*, a portrait that the researches of the biographer have been able to substantiate but little to augment." Ernest Campbell Mossner, "Philosophy and Biography: The Case of David Hume," *Philosophical Review* 59.2 (April 1950), 200–201.

78. This aspect of the *Letter* has been stressed in Schliesser, "Obituary of a Vain Philosopher," especially 347–52.

tion to give an "account of the behaviour of our late excellent friend," and he concludes with a character sketch of "our most excellent, and never to be forgotten friend."[79] In fact, he uses the word "friend" a remarkable seventeen times within the short work. Hume's comportment toward his friends and his great capacity for friendship were, according to Smith's depiction, among the principal proofs of the goodness of his character, and the friendships themselves were in turn among the chief rewards that he derived from this good character. The *Letter* thus illustrates and reinforces the claim that both Hume and Smith make elsewhere that friendship is a central and indeed indispensable component of a good and happy life.[80] The work also, by its very nature, calls attention to Hume and Smith's own friendship, and unobtrusively proposes it as a model of what a friendship should look like. This seems to be the essence of the somewhat cryptic claim of Dugald Stewart, Smith's contemporary and first biographer, that theirs "was a friendship on both sides founded on the admiration of genius, and the love of simplicity; and, which forms an interesting circumstance in the history of each of these eminent men, from the ambition which both have shewn to record it to posterity."[81]

Above all, the *Letter* was an attempt to vindicate Hume's reputation and secure his legacy in a world that was frequently hostile to him and almost always hostile to his ideas. In the context in which Smith wrote the work this meant affirming, in the face of nearly universal sentiment to the contrary, that a skeptic could both live and die well. Smith was well aware of the importance that many were attaching to the manner of Hume's death, and (like Hume himself) he wanted Hume to prove the critics wrong. "Since we must lose our friend," he told Wedderburn, "the most agreable thing that can happen is that he dyes as a man of sense ought to do."[82] Smith's description of Hume as a paragon of wisdom and virtue and his

79. See pp. 45 and 50 in this volume.

80. See, for instance, Hume's statement that "friendship is the chief joy of human life" and Smith's claim that the esteem and affection of one's friends constitutes "the chief part of human happiness." David Hume, *An Enquiry Concerning Human Understanding*, ed. Tom L. Beauchamp (Oxford: Clarendon Press, [1748] 2000), 1.20, 105; and Adam Smith, *The Theory of Moral Sentiments*, ed. D. D. Raphael and A. L. Macfie (Indianapolis: Liberty Fund, [1759–90] 1982), I.ii.5.1, 41; see also ibid., VI.ii.1.18, 224–25.

81. Dugald Stewart, *Account of the Life and Writings of Adam Smith, LL.D.*, ed. I. S. Ross, in Adam Smith, *Essays on Philosophical Subjects* (Indianapolis: Liberty Fund, [1794] 1980), 273.

82. See p. 56 in this volume.

constant references to Hume's cheerfulness and equanimity in his final months and days are difficult to read as anything other than a deliberate challenge to the devout. To be sure, Smith softened the antireligious barb in their banter about Charon, but he still chose to make this story, which was certain to cause offense, the centerpiece of the work. In discussing Hume's death Smith does not even allude to God, the soul, or the afterlife, any more than Hume himself had in *My Own Life*.

At least implicitly, then, the *Letter* is also a defense of the morality of a life without religion. In *The Theory of Moral Sentiments* Smith had suggested that religious faith offers comfort in the face of death as well as consolation for those who are wronged or wrongly judged here on earth.[83] Hume knew that his death was imminent and was frequently misjudged, but the *Letter* makes clear that he had no need for otherworldly comforts and consolations. Smith also argued in his first book that belief in God and an afterlife often helps to buttress morality.[84] Even there he never went so far as to suggest that religion is an *indispensable* component of a virtuous life, but the *Letter* establishes just how dispensable it is: the individual whom Smith regarded as "approaching as nearly to the idea of a perfectly wise and virtuous man, as perhaps the nature of human frailty will permit" was a religious skeptic.[85]

## REACTION

Publishing the *Letter to Strahan* was a brave act, especially given Smith's perennial aversion to public controversy. For the pious it was obnoxious enough that Hume remained a skeptic to the end, but they had long since written him off as an incorrigible infidel in any case. The greater outrage was that Smith, a widely respected former professor of moral philosophy, proceeded to rub their noses in it. He paid for it in spades. Smith later claimed that "a single, and as, I thought a very harmless Sheet of paper, which I happened to Write concerning the death of our late friend Mr Hume, brought upon me ten times more abuse than the very violent at-

83. See, for instance, Smith, *The Theory of Moral Sentiments*, III.2.12, 120–21; and III.2.33, 131–32.

84. See, for instance, ibid., III.5.3–7, 163–66.

85. See p. 51 in this volume.

tack I had made upon the whole commercial system of Great Britain."[86] Virtually all Smith scholars are familiar with this line because of the colorful reference to *The Wealth of Nations*—a book that, it is important to remember, was published just a year before the *Letter*—but far fewer know the precise nature and extent of the abuse that Smith faced as a consequence of his tribute to his friend.

Not everyone was offended, of course. Hume's other friends, who were in the best position to corroborate Smith's character sketch, were entirely persuaded by it. Hugh Blair—who was a minister, recall—wrote to Strahan: "Poor David! What an irreparable blank does he make amongst us here [in Edinburgh]. Taking him all in all, we shall never see the like. Indeed I cannot but agree with what Adam Smith says of him in the last sentence of his printed letter to you."[87] Hume and Smith also had one overeager defender named Samuel Jackson Pratt, who opened his effusive *Apology for the Life and Writings of David Hume* with the exceedingly inflated pronouncement: "David Hume is dead! Never were the pillars of Orthodoxy so desperately shaken, as they are now, by that event."[88] (Pratt too immediately came under fire.) In most circles, however, the reaction was very different. As John Ramsay of Ochtertyre writes, the *Letter to Strahan* "gave very great offence, and made [Smith] henceforth be regarded as an avowed sceptic, to the no small regret of many who revered his character and admired his writings. That his friend was an amiable philosopher of great parts and greater eloquence was not disputed. But when Dr Smith declared without any qualification that 'he had always considered Mr Hume, both in his lifetime and since his death, as approaching as nearly to the idea of a perfectly wise and virtuous man as perhaps the nature of human frailty would permit,' everybody was astonished that a man who had once been a professor should have expressed himself in these terms. It went so far as to affirm that it mattered not what speculative opinions men might entertain—a proposition which shocked every sober Christian."[89]

---

86. Adam Smith to Andreas Holt, 26 October 1780, in CAS, 251.

87. Hugh Blair to William Strahan, 10 April 1778, in Hill, *Letters of David Hume to William Strahan*, xl n. 1.

88. [Samuel Jackson Pratt,] *An Apology for the Life and Writings of David Hume, Esq.: With a Parallel Between Him and the Late Lord Chesterfield: To Which Is Added an Address to One of the People Called Christians, By Way of Reply to His Letter to Adam Smith* (London: Fielding and Walker, 1777), 1.

89. Ramsay of Ochtertyre, *Scotland and Scotsmen in the Eighteenth Century*, 466–67.

The attack was led by George Horne, who was at the time the Vice-Chancellor of Oxford University, the President of Oxford's Magdalen College, and a chaplain in ordinary to King George III.[90] Horne was a staunch defender of "high church" Anglicanism, and would later become Dean of Canterbury (1781–1790) and then conclude his career as Bishop of Norwich (1790–1792). His open (but anonymous) letter to Smith, bearing the derisive title *A Letter to Adam Smith LL.D. on the Life, Death, and Philosophy of His Friend David Hume Esq., By One of the People Called Christians*, is included in this volume.[91] Horne's basic point, which he belabors with much sarcasm, was one that would recur time and again in the course of the controversy: Hume could not have been truly virtuous because he was an atheist, and sought to spread his atheism to others through his writings.[92] Horne accepts that Hume may have been "a social agreeable person, of a convivial turn, told a good story, and played well at 'his favourite game of whist,'" but he insists that Hume could not have been—as Smith claimed—genuinely gentle mannered, good natured, compassionate, generous, and charitable "when he so often sate down calmly and deliberately to obliterate from the hearts of the human species every trace of the knowledge of GOD and his dispensations; all faith in his kind providence, and fatherly protection; all hope of enjoying his grace and favour, here, or hereafter; all love of him, and of their brethren for his sake; all the patience under tribulation, all the comforts, in time of sorrow, derived from these fruitful and perennial sources."[93]

Above all Horne upbraids Smith for reporting, and apparently endorsing, Hume's nonchalant attitude toward death and the afterlife. Smith seems to want to persuade his readers, Horne says, "that atheism is the only cordial for low spirits, and the proper antidote against the fear of death. But, surely, he who can reflect, with complacency, on a

---

90. Given Horne's position at Oxford, he may have also been provoked by Smith's recently published comment that "in the university of Oxford, the greater part of the publick professors have, for these many years, given up altogether even the pretence of teaching." Adam Smith, *An Inquiry into the Nature and Causes of the Wealth of Nations*, ed. R. H. Campbell, A. S. Skinner, and W. B. Todd (Indianapolis: Liberty Fund [1776], 1981), V.i.f.8, 761. Smith studied at Oxford's Balliol College from 1740 to 1746, but found the instruction exceedingly uninspiring.

91. See pp. 59–73.

92. A prominent nineteenth-century biographer of Smith remarks that Horne thereby "beg[s] the whole question he raises." John Rae, *Life of Adam Smith* (New York: Augustus M. Kelley, [1895] 1965), 312.

93. See pp. 61 and 64 in this volume.

friend . . . amusing himself with LUCIAN, WHIST, and CHARON, at his death, may smile over BABYLON in ruins; esteem the earthquake, which destroyed LISBON, an agreeable occurrence; and congratulate the hardened PHARAOH, on his overthrow in the Red sea." If Smith had been a true friend, or even a decent person, in other words, he would have pleaded with Hume to seek eternal salvation, rather than playing cards or joking about Charon, and he certainly would not have advertised—indeed paraded—Hume's impious attitude to all the world. Horne concludes that their joint conduct in this instance is a sure sign of the "baneful and pestilential influences of false philosophy on the human heart."[94] The work was first published in April 1777, and it was sufficiently popular that two more editions were printed later that year, followed by a half dozen more over the next few decades.

Horne's pamphlet was the most prominent rejoinder to the *Letter to Strahan*, but there were dozens of others over the next few years in various journals, books, sermons, and even poems.[95] The most substantial response, next to Horne's, came in an extended letter to the *Weekly Magazine, or Edinburgh Amusement* a few weeks after the journal reprinted the *Letter to Strahan*; this letter too is included in this volume.[96] The author, who signed the letter only "E. M.," wonders aloud whether the *Letter to Strahan* could have been anything other than satirical. While Smith doubtless meant to produce "a panegyric upon his friend," this commentator claims, in fact his portrait of "a man of distinguished intellectual powers acting the fool at his end" can only "expose Mr H–'s memory to the pity, if not to the contempt, of the truly wise and virtuous part of mankind."[97] Like Horne, he returns several times to Smith's concluding statement about Hume's wisdom and virtue. Also like Horne, he suggests that nothing could be "more frivolous, more childish, more indecently wanton and presumptuous in a dying man, perceiving himself on the verge of time, than Mr H–'s sportful dialogue with *Charon*" and that Hume's example cannot come close to comparing "for true greatness, with the meanest Christian *dying in faith*."[98]

94. See pp. 24–25 in this volume.

95. For a useful compilation of a number of these, see James Fieser, ed., *Early Responses to Hume*, second edition (Bristol, UK: Thoemmes Continuum, 2005), vol. 9, 383 ff.

96. See pp. 75–80.

97. See p. 75 in this volume.

98. See pp. 77 and 79 in this volume.

The present volume concludes with an amusing rejoinder to "E. M.," also published as a letter to the *Weekly Magazine, or Edinburgh Amusement*, under the name "Idem."[99] This letter defends Hume and Smith against the attack of "E. M." under the guise of pretending to join in the attack. Via unconcealed irony the author praises Hume's character and writings, and he suggests that there is nothing particularly immoral or indecent about joking as one approaches death, as Hume did in his conversation with Smith about Charon.

The inclusion of a defense of Hume and Smith in this volume should not, however, obscure the fact that their critics vastly outnumbered their supporters. Some of the more colorful jabs came from none other than James Boswell, who knew both philosophers reasonably well. Boswell rented Hume's apartment in the Lawnmarket when Hume moved to the New Town in 1771, for instance, and his account of his final interview with Hume is justifiably famous.[100] Earlier, Boswell had gone to Glasgow University for a brief time for the express purpose of taking Smith's moral philosophy course, and he remained quite fond of Smith for many years.[101] Nonetheless, Boswell considered the *Letter to Strahan* a piece of "daring effrontery" and an example of the "poisonous productions with which this age is infested." He beseeched his friend and mentor, Samuel Johnson, to "step forth" and "knock Hume's and Smith's heads together, and make vain and ostentatious infidelity exceedingly ridiculous. Would it not," he pleaded, "be worth your while to crush such noxious weeds in the moral garden?"[102] Boswell remarks elsewhere that when he read the *Letter*'s concluding sentence, "delivered by my old Professor of Moral Philosophy, I could not help exclaiming with the Psalmist, 'Surely I have now more understanding than my teachers!'"[103] More than two years after the

99. See pp. 81–87.

100. See James Boswell, *Boswell in Extremes, 1776–1778*, ed. Charles McC. Weis and Frederick A. Pottle (New York: McGraw-Hill, 1970), 11–13.

101. See James Boswell to John Johnston of Grange, 11 January 1760, in *The Correspondence of James Boswell and John Johnston of Grange*, ed. Ralph S. Walker (New York: McGraw-Hill, 1966), 7.

102. James Boswell, *The Life of Samuel Johnson*, ed. David Womersley (New York: Penguin, [1791] 2008), 585.

103. James Boswell, *Journal of a Tour to the Hebrides with Samuel Johnson, LL.D.*, ed. Frederick A. Pottle and Charles H. Bennett (New York: McGraw-Hill, [1785] 1961), 18. Boswell was also of the opinion that the *Letter to Strahan* was "shattered by the sharp shot of Dr. *Horne* of *Oxford's* wit, in the character of 'One of the People called Christians.'" Ibid.

*Letter* was published Boswell still felt aggrieved enough to express his indignation to Smith: "I fairly told him that I did not like his having praised David Hume so much. He went off to the board huffed"—they were at the customs house, where Smith worked in his later years—"yet affecting to treat my censure as foolish. I did not care how he took it. Since his absurd eulogium on Hume . . . I have had no desire to be much with him."[104]

Boswell's friend William Johnson Temple, for his part, thought Smith should be ashamed of himself: "A professor (once) of Moral Philosophy, an instructor of youth, ought to be ashamed to own so intimate a connection & so blamable an admiration of a man who gloried & died in the disbelief of a Providence & a Futurity. I should think he must have hurt his character greatly & essentially by his publick avowal of this man. It is equal to adopting all his worst opinions both in Religion & Government."[105] If Boswell is to be believed, even Edmund Burke, a great admirer of Smith's, deemed the *Letter to Strahan* a laughable attempt to spread the gospel of infidelity: "Talking of David Hume, Mr. Burke laughed at his life [i.e., *My Own Life*] and at Smith's appendix 'most virtuous,' etc. 'This,' said he, 'is said for the credit of their church, and the members of no church use more art for its credit . . . Here was a man at a great age, who had been preparing all along to die without showing fear, does it, and rout is made about it. Men in general die easily.'"[106]

Nor did the controversy die down quickly. Well over a decade later, in a sermon delivered just months before Smith's death, John Wesley, the founder of the Methodist movement, thundered (apparently to Hume's ghost): "What think you now of Charon? Has he ferried you over [the] Styx? . . . At length you know, it is a fearful thing to fall into the hands of the living God!"[107] Still later, in the early nineteenth century, stories began to circulate that, despite the accounts given by Smith, Black, Boswell, and several others of Hume's cheerfulness and serenity during

104. James Boswell, *Boswell: Laird of Auchinleck, 1778–1782*, ed. Joseph W. Reed and Frederick A. Pottle (New York: McGraw Hill, 1977), 135; see also 255.

105. William Johnson Temple to James Boswell, 21 March 1777, in *The Correspondence of James Boswell and William Johnson Temple, 1756–1795, Volume 1: 1756–1777*, ed. Thomas Crawford (New Haven: Yale University Press, 1997), 433.

106. Boswell, *Boswell in Extremes*, 270.

107. John Wesley, "On the Deceitfulness of the Human Heart," in *The Works of the Rev. John Wesley, A. M.*, third edition (London: John Mason, [1790] 1829), vol. 7, 342.

his final weeks, he was in fact filled with anguish, fear, and remorse during much of this period, and only put on a good face while visitors were present.[108] Not to put too fine a point on it, Smith was loudly called a liar—or, at best, the dupe of Hume's ploy to portray himself as more tranquil than he really was in the face of death. All of the sources of this rumor were, predictably, fervently religious, and they all attribute Hume's alleged anguish to his irreligion rather than to his physical ailments. One of the accounts even extended the torments to include Smith. According to a thirdhand report published in 1852, Smith extracted a promise from Hume during his final days that after his death, "if it were in his power, to meet [him] in the shady avenue of 'the Meadows,' behind George-square"—south of Edinburgh's Old Town, adjacent to the university—in order to "tell the secrets of the world unknown." Such was the effect of this pledge on Smith, the report has it, that "no persuasion would induce him to walk in the meadows after sunset."[109] How far to credit such stories can safely be left to the reader to determine, but they do testify to the continuing impact that Hume's death, and Smith's account of it, had on religious sensibilities, even many decades after the fact. Indeed, nearly a century after the *Letter to Strahan* was published one prolific author of religious tomes was still sufficiently incensed by it to proclaim that he knew "no more lamentable evidence of the weakness and folly of irreligion and infidelity" in "all the range of English literature."[110]

While Smith himself regarded (or affected to regard) the *Letter to Strahan* as "a very harmless Sheet of paper," then, clearly many others did not see it that way.[111] And it is important to remember that all of this invective ensued even after he omitted some of his and Hume's more offensive remarks. There is no telling how much obloquy he would have endured had the critics known that Hume hoped for "the pleasure of seeing the churches shut up, and the Clergy sent about their business" and that Smith proclaimed that Hume died "with more real resignation to the necessary

108. See the stories collected in Fieser, *Early Responses to Hume*, vol. 9, 319–32 and 424–25.

109. Alexander Haldane, *Memoirs of the Lives of Robert Haldane of Airthrey, and of His Brother, James Alexander Haldane* (London: Hamilton, Adams, and Co., 1852), 581–82.

110. John M. Lowrie, *The Life of David* (Philadelphia: Presbyterian Board of Publication, 1869), 418.

111. Adam Smith to Andreas Holt, 26 October 1780, in CAS, 251.

course of things, than any whining Christian ever dyed with pretended resignation to the will of God."[112]

Though Smith later commented that the *Letter* brought on him ten times more abuse than *The Wealth of Nations*, he never retracted the claims he made in it, never expressed regret for having published it, and never responded to the critics. As Greig put it, "he had delivered his opinion of 'le bon David,' and he stood by it, without another word. Adam Smith knew his man."[113]

112. See pp. 56 and 55 in this volume, respectively.

113. Greig, *David Hume*, 414.

# Chronology

**1776**

| | |
|---|---|
| January 4 | Hume draws up a will, naming Smith his literary executor |
| March 9 | Publication of Smith's *The Wealth of Nations* |
| April 18 | Date of Hume's *My Own Life*; soon afterward Hume leaves Edinburgh for London and then Bath |
| April 23 | Hume and Smith meet at Morpeth |
| July 3 | Hume returns to Edinburgh |
| August 7 | Hume amends his will to make Strahan his literary executor |
| August 8 | Hume and Smith's conversation about Charon |
| August 22 | Smith proposes to Hume to "add a few lines to your account of your own life" |
| August 23 | Hume gives Smith "entire liberty to make what Additions you please to the account of my Life" |
| August 25 | Hume's death |
| October 7 | Smith sends a draft of the *Letter to Strahan* to Joseph Black and Hume's brother for comment |
| November 9 | Date of Smith's *Letter to Strahan* |
| November 13 | Smith sends the *Letter to Strahan* to Strahan |

## 1777

| | |
|---|---|
| January | Publication of *My Own Life* and the *Letter to Strahan* in *Scots Magazine* |
| March 11 | Publication of *My Own Life* and the *Letter to Strahan* as a pamphlet by Strahan |
| April | Publication of Horne's *Letter to Adam Smith* |
| April 24 | Publication of the "Remarks on Dr. Adam Smith's Letter to Mr. Strahan" |
| May 8 | Publication of the "Observations Relative to the Late David Hume" |

# A Note on the Texts

The copytext for David Hume's *My Own Life* is the version that was authorized by Smith, which was included in *The Life of David Hume, Esq., Written By Himself* (London: Printed for W. Strahan; and T. Cadell, in the Strand, 1777). This version differs in many matters of punctuation and spelling from the one published in the January 1777 issue of the *Scots Magazine*, as well as from the original manuscript, which is now housed at the National Library of Scotland (MS. 23159, no. 23). For a critical edition of the manuscript, including a full facsimile, see *David Hume: My Own Life*, edited by Iain Gordon Brown (Edinburgh: Royal Society of Edinburgh, 2014).

There is no surviving manuscript of the *Letter from Adam Smith, LL.D. to William Strahan, Esq.* Here too the copytext is the version that was included in *The Life of David Hume, Esq., Written By Himself* (London: Printed for W. Strahan; and T. Cadell, in the Strand, 1777). Once again, the version published in the January 1777 issue of the *Scots Magazine* differs from this one in many matters of punctuation and spelling, including the incorporation of the indefinite article into the title: *A Letter from Adam Smith, LL.D. to William Strahan, Esq.*

The letter from James Edmonstoune to David Hume, August 7, 1776, is part of the Royal Society of Edinburgh's David Hume Bequest, held on deposit at the National Library of Scotland (MS. 23155, no. V, 7), and is included here with their kind permission. The transcription differs in minor respects from the one in HL II, 331 n. 1.

The letter from Adam Smith to Alexander Wedderburn, August 14, 1776, is housed at the University of Glasgow Library, Special Collections (MS. Gen. 510/47), and is included here with their kind permission. The transcription differs in minor respects from the one in CAS, 203–4.

The copytext for George Horne's anonymous public letter is the first published edition: *A Letter to Adam Smith LL.D. on the Life, Death, and Philosophy of His Friend David Hume Esq., By One of the People Called Christians* (Oxford: Clarendon, 1777). Later editions incorporated an additional footnote into the postscript, which is noted in the present volume, along with changes in punctuation and spelling throughout, which are not noted. I have reproduced Horne's own notes using lettered footnotes in this volume, alongside the numbered editorial notes.

The final two items were both published in the periodical *The Weekly Magazine, or Edinburgh Amusement*. The first, signed only "E. M.," appeared as "REMARKS *on Dr* ADAM SMITH's *Letter to Mr* STRAHAN, *on the Death of* DAVID HUME, *Esq*; *To the* PUBLISHER *of the* WEEKLY MAGAZINE" in the 24 April 1777 issue (vol. 36), 139–41. The second, signed "IDEM.," appeared as "OBSERVATIONS *relative to the late* DAVID HUME, *Esq*; *To the* PUBLISHER *of the* WEEKLY MAGAZINE," in the 8 May 1777 issue (vol. 36), 193–96.

# My Own Life

## David Hume

It is difficult for a man to speak long of himself without vanity; therefore, I shall be short. It may be thought an instance of vanity that I pretend at all to write my life; but this Narrative shall contain little more than the History of my Writings; as, indeed, almost all my life has been spent in literary pursuits and occupations. The first success of most of my writings was not such as to be an object of vanity.

I was born the 26th of April 1711, old style,[1] at Edinburgh. I was of a good family, both by father and mother: my father's family is a branch of the Earl of Home's, or Hume's;[2] and my ancestors had been proprietors of the estate, which my brother possesses,[3] for several generations. My mother was daughter of Sir David Falconer, President of the College of Justice: the title of Lord Halkerton came by succession to her brother.

My family, however, was not rich, and being myself a younger brother, my patrimony, according to the mode of my country, was of course very slender. My father, who passed for a man of parts, died when I was an infant, leaving me, with an elder brother and a sister, under the care of our mother, a woman of singular merit, who, though young and handsome, devoted herself entirely to the rearing and educating of her children. I

1. In 1752 Britain switched from the Julian calendar (which was thereafter referred to as "Old Style") to the Gregorian calendar ("New Style"). 26 April 1711, Old Style, is equivalent to 7 May 1711, New Style.

2. Hume changed the spelling of his given last name, Home, to match the pronunciation while in England in 1734.

3. Hume's brother, John Home (1709–1786), maintained the family estate at Ninewells, south of Edinburgh, near the border with England.

passed through the ordinary course of education with success, and was seized very early with a passion for literature, which has been the ruling passion of my life, and the great source of my enjoyments.[4] My studious disposition, my sobriety, and my industry, gave my family a notion that the law was a proper profession for me; but I found an unsurmountable aversion to every thing but the pursuits of philosophy and general learning; and while they fancied I was poring upon Voet and Vinnius,[5] Cicero and Virgil were the authors which I was secretly devouring.

My very slender fortune, however, being unsuitable to this plan of life, and my health being a little broken by my ardent application, I was tempted, or rather forced, to make a very feeble trial for entering into a more active scene of life. In 1734, I went to Bristol, with some recommendations to eminent merchants, but in a few months found that scene totally unsuitable to me. I went over to France, with a view of prosecuting my studies in a country retreat; and I there laid that plan of life, which I have steadily and successfully pursued. I resolved to make a very rigid frugality supply my deficiency of fortune, to maintain unimpaired my independency, and to regard every object as contemptible, except the improvement of my talents in literature.

During my retreat in France, first at Reims, but chiefly at La Fleche, in Anjou, I composed my *Treatise of Human Nature*. After passing three years very agreeably in that country, I came over to London in 1737. In the end of 1738, I published my Treatise,[6] and immediately went down to my mother and my brother, who lived at his country-house, and was employing himself very judiciously and successfully in the improvement of his fortune.

Never literary attempt was more unfortunate than my Treatise of Human Nature. It fell *dead-born from the press*, without reaching such dis-

---

4. Hume also refers to his "ruling passion" in the final paragraph, where he identifies that passion as "my love of literary fame" (see p. 43 in this volume). The phrase "ruling passion" was popularized by Alexander Pope, particularly his *Essay on Man* (1733) and *Epistle to Lord Cobham* (1734). See Alexander Pope, *The Major Works*, ed. Pat Rogers (Oxford: Oxford University Press, 2006), 284, 319, 324, 326.

5. Johannes Voet (1647–1713) and Arnold Vinnius (1588–1657) were both Dutch jurists. Voet's commentary on Justinian's *Pandects* and Vinnius's commentary on Justinian's *Institutes* were foundational works in Scottish civil law.

6. Books 1 and 2 of *A Treatise of Human Nature* were in fact published in 1739; Book 3 appeared in 1740.

tinction, as even to excite a murmur among the zealots.[7] But being naturally of a cheerful and sanguine temper, I very soon recovered the blow, and prosecuted with great ardour my studies in the country. In 1742, I printed at Edinburgh the first part of my Essays[8]: the work was favourably received, and soon made me entirely forget my former disappointment. I continued with my mother and brother in the country, and in that time recovered the knowledge of the Greek language, which I had too much neglected in my early youth.

In 1745, I received a letter from the Marquis of Annandale, inviting me to come and live with him in England; I found also, that the friends and family of that young nobleman were desirous of putting him under my care and direction, for the state of his mind and health required it.[9]—I lived with him a twelvemonth. My appointments during that time made a considerable accession to my small fortune. I then received an invitation from General St. Clair to attend him as a secretary to his expedition, which was at first meant against Canada, but ended in an incursion on the coast of France.[10] Next year, to wit, 1747, I received an invitation from the General to attend him in the same station in his military embassy to the courts of Vienna and Turin. I then wore the uniform of an officer, and was introduced at these courts as aid-de-camp to the general, along with Sir Harry Erskine and Captain Grant, now General Grant.[11] These two years were almost the only interruptions which my studies have received during the course of my life: I passed them agreeably, and in good company; and my appointments, with my frugality, had made me reach a fortune, which I called independent, though most of my friends were inclined to smile when I said so; in short, I was now master of near a thousand pounds.

---

7. The italicized phrase derives from Alexander Pope's declaration that "All, all but Truth, drops dead-born from the Press, / Like the last Gazette, or the last address." Pope, *Epilogue to the Satires* (1738), in *The Major Works*, 407.

8. The first volume of Hume's *Essays Moral and Political* was in fact published in 1741; volume two appeared in 1742.

9. George, 3rd Marquess of Annandale (1720–1792), was declared legally insane a few years after Hume left his employ.

10. Lieutenant-General James St. Clair (1688–1762) was a distant relation of Hume's. The expedition to Brittany, part of the War of the Austrian Succession, was little more than a diversion designed to draw off French troops from the heavier fighting in Flanders.

11. Sir Henry Erskine (1710–1765), St. Clair's nephew, was a military officer and later a politician. James Grant of Ballindalloch (1720–1806) was a military officer and later colonial governor of East Florida; he attained the rank of general in 1775, and would go on to play a considerable role in the American Revolutionary War.

I had always entertained a notion, that my want of success in publishing the Treatise of Human Nature, had proceeded more from the manner than the matter, and that I had been guilty of a very usual indiscretion, in going to the press too early. I, therefore, cast the first part of that work anew in the Enquiry concerning Human Understanding,[12] which was published while I was at Turin. But this piece was at first little more successful than the Treatise of Human Nature. On my return from Italy, I had the mortification to find all England in a ferment, on account of Dr. Middleton's Free Enquiry,[13] while my performance was entirely overlooked and neglected. A new edition, which had been published at London of my Essays, moral and political, met not with a much better reception.

Such is the force of natural temper, that these disappointments made little or no impression on me. I went down in 1749, and lived two years with my brother at his country-house, for my mother was now dead. I there composed the second part of my Essays, which I called Political Discourses, and also my Enquiry concerning the Principles of Morals, which is another part of my treatise that I cast anew. Meanwhile, my bookseller, A. Millar,[14] informed me, that my former publications (all but the unfortunate Treatise) were beginning to be the subject of conversation; that the sale of them was gradually increasing, and that new editions were demanded. Answers by Reverends, and Right Reverends, came out two or three in a year; and I found, by Dr. Warburton's[15] railing, that the books were beginning to be esteemed in good company. However, I had fixed a resolution, which I inflexibly maintained, never to reply to any body; and not being very irascible in my temper, I have easily kept myself clear of all literary squabbles. These symptoms of a rising reputation gave me

---

12. *An Enquiry Concerning Human Understanding* (now often referred to as the *First Enquiry*) was originally published under the title *Philosophical Essays Concerning Human Understanding* (1748).

13. Conyers Middleton (1683–1750) was a controversial Anglican clergyman who often strayed from orthodoxy. His *A Free Inquiry into the Miraculous Powers, Which Are Supposed to Have Subsisted in the Christian Church, From the Earliest Ages through Several Successive Centuries* (1749) cast doubt on the reality of the miracles that had allegedly taken place since the time of the apostles. Hume's more sweeping attack on the idea of miracles appears in section 10 of the *First Enquiry.*

14. Andrew Millar (1705–1768) was, like William Strahan, a Scot based in London and a leading figure in the book industry. He often worked in partnership with Strahan, and he also published Smith's *The Theory of Moral Sentiments.*

15. William Warburton (1698–1779), at this time an Anglican priest, later became Bishop of Gloucester. He was a leading religious controversialist and a longtime opponent of Hume's.

encouragement, as I was ever more disposed to see the favourable than unfavourable side of things; a turn of mind which it is more happy to possess, than to be born to an estate of ten thousand a year.

In 1751, I removed from the country to the town, the true scene for a man of letters. In 1752, were published at Edinburgh, where I then lived, my Political Discourses, the only work of mine that was successful on the first publication. It was well received abroad and at home. In the same year was published at London, my Enquiry concerning the Principles of Morals[16]; which, in my own opinion (who ought not to judge on that subject), is of all my writings, historical, philosophical, or literary, incomparably the best. It came unnoticed and unobserved into the world.

In 1752, the Faculty of Advocates chose me their Librarian, an office from which I received little or no emolument, but which gave me the command of a large library. I then formed the plan of writing the History of England; but being frightened with the notion of continuing a narrative through a period of 1700 years, I commenced with the accession of the House of Stuart, an epoch when, I thought, the misrepresentations of faction began chiefly to take place.[17] I was, I own, sanguine in my expectations of the success of this work. I thought that I was the only historian, that had at once neglected present power, interest, and authority, and the cry of popular prejudices; and as the subject was suited to every capacity, I expected proportional applause. But miserable was my disappointment: I was assailed by one cry of reproach, disapprobation, and even detestation; English, Scotch, and Irish, Whig and Tory, churchman and sectary, freethinker and religionist, patriot and courtier, united in their rage against the man, who had presumed to shed a generous tear for the fate of Charles I. and the Earl of Strafford; and after the first ebullitions of their fury were over, what was still more mortifying, the book seemed to sink into oblivion. Mr. Millar told me, that in a twelvemonth he sold only forty-five copies of it. I scarcely, indeed, heard of one man in the three kingdoms, considerable for rank or letters, that could endure the book. I must only except the primate of England, Dr. Herring, and the primate of Ireland,

16. While the *Political Discourses* was published in 1752, as Hume suggests, *An Enquiry Concerning the Principles of Morals* (the *Second Enquiry*) was in fact published in 1751.

17. The first volume of what was originally titled *The History of Great Britain*—which would eventually become the fifth of the six volumes of *The History of England*—focused on the reigns of James I and Charles I (1603–1649), and was published in 1754.

Dr. Stone, which seem two odd exceptions.[18] These dignified prelates separately sent me messages not to be discouraged.

I was, however, I confess, discouraged; and had not the war been at that time breaking out between France and England,[19] I had certainly retired to some provincial town of the former kingdom, have changed my name, and never more have returned to my native country. But as this scheme was not now practicable, and the subsequent volume was considerably advanced, I resolved to pick up courage and to persevere.

In this interval, I published at London my Natural History of Religion, along with some other small pieces[20]: its public entry was rather obscure, except only that Dr. Hurd wrote a pamphlet against it, with all the illiberal petulance, arrogance, and scurrility, which distinguish the Warburtonian school.[21] This pamphlet gave me some consolation for the otherwise indifferent reception of my performance.

In 1756, two years after the fall of the first volume, was published the second volume of my History, containing the period from the death of Charles I. till the Revolution.[22] This performance happened to give less displeasure to the Whigs, and was better received. It not only rose itself, but helped to buoy up its unfortunate brother.

But though I had been taught by experience, that the Whig party were in possession of bestowing all places, both in the state and in literature, I was so little inclined to yield to their senseless clamour, that in above a hundred alterations, which farther study, reading, or reflection engaged me to make in the reigns of the two first Stuarts, I have made all of them

18. Thomas Herring (1693–1757) was Archbishop of Canterbury (and therefore "Primate of All England") and George Stone (1708–1764) was Archbishop of Armagh (and therefore "Primate of All Ireland").

19. The Seven Years' War lasted from 1756 to 1763.

20. *The Natural History of Religion* was the centerpiece of Hume's *Four Dissertations* (1757); the volume also included "Of the Passions," "Of Tragedy," and "Of the Standard of Taste."

21. Richard Hurd (1720–1808), at this time an Anglican priest and later Bishop of Worcester, was a close friend and ally of William Warburton. The pamphlet that Hume mentions, *Remarks on Mr David Hume's Essay on the Natural History of Religion: Addressed to the Rev. Dr. Warburton* (1757), which was published anonymously, in fact consisted mostly of Warburton's trenchant observations in the margins of Hume's *Four Dissertations*, which Hurd compiled into a pamphlet.

22. The second volume of *The History of Great Britain* (1756)—which became the sixth of *The History of England*—covered, as Hume notes, the period from 1649–1689.

invariably to the Tory side. It is ridiculous to consider the English constitution before that period as a regular plan of liberty.

In 1759, I published my History of the House of Tudor.[23] The clamour against this performance was almost equal to that against the History of the two first Stuarts. The reign of Elizabeth was particularly obnoxious. But I was now callous against the impressions of public folly, and continued very peaceably and contentedly in my retreat at Edinburgh, to finish, in two volumes, the more early part of the English History, which I gave to the public in 1761, with tolerable, and but tolerable success.[24]

But, notwithstanding this variety of winds and seasons, to which my writings had been exposed, they had still been making such advances, that the copy-money given me by the booksellers, much exceeded any thing formerly known in England; I was become not only independent, but opulent. I retired to my native country of Scotland, determined never more to set my foot out of it; and retaining the satisfaction of never having preferred a request to one great man, or even making advances of friendship to any of them. As I was now turned of fifty, I thought of passing all the rest of my life in this philosophical manner, when I received, in 1763, an invitation from the Earl of Hertford, with whom I was not in the least acquainted, to attend him on his embassy to Paris, with a near prospect of being appointed secretary to the embassy; and, in the meanwhile, of performing the functions of that office.[25] This offer, however inviting, I at first declined, both because I was reluctant to begin connexions with the great, and because I was afraid that the civilities and gay company of Paris, would prove disagreeable to a person of my age and humour: but on his lordship's repeating the invitation, I accepted of it. I have every reason, both of pleasure and interest, to think myself happy in my connex-

23. The two-volume *The History of England, under the House of Tudor* (1759)—which became the third and fourth volumes of the complete *The History of England*—covered the Tudor era (1485–1603).

24. The final two volumes of *The History of England* (1761)—which now became the first two volumes in the six-volume set—covered the long period from the invasion of Julius Caesar all the way up to the accession of Henry VII in 1485.

25. Francis Seymour-Conway, 1st Earl of Hertford (1718–1794), was a lifelong politician. He was the British ambassador to France from 1763–1765. Hume served as his de facto Secretary for most of that time, though he would not attain the official title (and full salary) until July 1765.

ions with that nobleman, as well as afterwards with his brother, General Conway.[26]

Those who have not seen the strange effects of modes, will never imagine the reception I met with at Paris, from men and women of all ranks and stations. The more I resiled from their excessive civilities, the more I was loaded with them. There is, however, a real satisfaction in living at Paris, from the great number of sensible, knowing, and polite company with which that city abounds above all places in the universe. I thought once of settling there for life.

I was appointed secretary to the embassy; and, in summer 1765, Lord Hertford left me, being appointed Lord Lieutenant of Ireland. I was *chargé d'affaires* till the arrival of the Duke of Richmond, towards the end of the year.[27] In the beginning of 1766, I left Paris, and next summer went to Edinburgh, with the same view as formerly, of burying myself in a philosophical retreat. I returned to that place, not richer, but with much more money, and a much larger income, by means of Lord Hertford's friendship, than I left it; and I was desirous of trying what superfluity could produce, as I had formerly made an experiment of a competency. But, in 1767, I received from Mr. Conway an invitation to be Undersecretary[28]; and this invitation, both the character of the person, and my connexions with Lord Hertford, prevented me from declining. I returned to Edinburgh in 1769, very opulent (for I possessed a revenue of 1000 l. a year), healthy, and though somewhat stricken in years, with the prospect of enjoying long my ease, and of seeing the increase of my reputation.

In spring 1775, I was struck with a disorder in my bowels, which at first gave me no alarm, but has since, as I apprehend it, become mortal and incurable.[29] I now reckon upon a speedy dissolution. I have suffered very little pain from my disorder; and what is more strange, have, not-

26. Henry Seymour Conway (1721–1795) was a prominent army general and politician. For Hume's "connexions" with him, see footnote 28 below.

27. As noted, Hume was officially appointed Secretary to the embassy in July 1765. Hertford left Paris near the end of that month, and from his departure through mid-November Hume was *chargé d'affaires*—essentially, the acting ambassador.

28. Conway became Secretary of State for the Northern Department—the body that handled diplomacy with Scotland, the northern European countries, and Russia—in 1766 and soon thereafter invited Hume to become his deputy or "Under-Secretary." Hume served in that role from February 1767 to January 1768.

29. Hume suffered from night fevers, internal bleeding, and severe diarrhea—probably the result of colon cancer, and perhaps also ulcerative colitis. For a modern diagnosis, see J.

withstanding the great decline of my person, never suffered a moment's abatement of my spirits; insomuch, that were I to name the period of my life, which I should most choose to pass over again, I might be tempted to point to this later period. I possess the same ardour as ever in study, and the same gaiety in company. I consider, besides, that a man of sixty-five, by dying, cuts off only a few years of infirmities; and though I see many symptoms of my literary reputation's breaking out at last with additional lustre, I knew that I could have but few years to enjoy it. It is difficult to be more detached from life than I am at present.

To conclude historically with my own character. I am, or rather was (for that is the style I must now use in speaking of myself, which emboldens me the more to speak my sentiments); I was, I say, a man of mild dispositions, of command of temper, of an open, social, and cheerful humour, capable of attachment, but little susceptible of enmity, and of great moderation in all my passions. Even my love of literary fame, my ruling passion, never soured my temper, notwithstanding my frequent disappointments. My company was not unacceptable to the young and careless, as well as to the studious and literary; and as I took a particular pleasure in the company of modest women, I had no reason to be displeased with the reception I met with from them. In a word, though most men any wise eminent, have found reason to complain of calumny, I never was touched, or even attacked by her baleful tooth: and though I wantonly exposed myself to the rage of both civil and religious factions, they seemed to be disarmed in my behalf of their wonted fury. My friends never had occasion to vindicate any one circumstance of my character and conduct: not but that the zealots, we may well suppose, would have been glad to invent and propagate any story to my disadvantage, but they could never find any which they thought would wear the face of probability. I cannot say there is no vanity in making this funeral oration of myself, but I hope it is not a misplaced one; and this is a matter of fact which is easily cleared and ascertained.

April 18, 1776.

---

Wilkinson, "The Last Illness of David Hume," *Proceedings of the Royal College of Physicians of Edinburgh* 18.1 (January 1988), 72–79.

# Letter from Adam Smith, LL.D. to William Strahan, Esq.

Kirkaldy, Fifeshire, Nov. 9, 1776.

DEAR SIR,

It is with a real, though a very melancholy pleasure, that I sit down to give you some account of the behaviour of our late excellent friend, Mr. Hume, during his last illness.

Though, in his own judgment, his disease was mortal and incurable, yet he allowed himself to be prevailed upon, by the entreaty of his friends, to try what might be the effects of a long journey. A few days before he set out, he wrote that account of his own life, which, together with his other papers, he has left to your care.[1] My account, therefore, shall begin where his ends.

He set out for London towards the end of April, and at Morpeth met with Mr. John Home and myself, who had both come down from London on purpose to see him, expecting to have found him at Edinburgh.[2] Mr. Home returned with him, and attended him during the whole of his stay in England, with that care and attention which might be expected from

1. See pp. 35–43 in this volume.

2. Morpeth is in northeast England, on the road between London and Edinburgh. In the eighteenth century Scots frequently spoke of "going down" or "coming down" from London north to Scotland; Hume uses a similar expression twice in *My Own Life* (see pp. 36 and 38 in this volume). John Home (1722–1808) was a playwright and a former Moderate minister in the Church of Scotland; he was forced to resign his ministry due to the religious controversy prompted by his tragedy *Douglas* (1756–1757). He was close friends with Smith and (especially) Hume. For Home's account of the fortuitous meeting at Morpeth, see Henry Mackenzie, *An Account of the Life and Writings of John Home, Esq.* (Edinburgh: Archibald Constable and Co., 1822), 168.

a temper so perfectly friendly and affectionate.[3] As I had written to my mother that she might expect me in Scotland, I was under the necessity of continuing my journey. His disease seemed to yield to exercise and change of air, and when he arrived in London, he was apparently in much better health than when he left Edinburgh. He was advised to go to Bath to drink the waters, which appeared for some time to have so good an effect upon him, that even he himself began to entertain, what he was not apt to do, a better opinion of his own health. His symptoms, however, soon returned with their usual violence, and from that moment he gave up all thoughts of recovery, but submitted with the utmost cheerfulness, and the most perfect complacency and resignation. Upon his return to Edinburgh, though he found himself much weaker, yet his cheerfulness never abated, and he continued to divert himself, as usual, with correcting his own works for a new edition, with reading books of amusement, with the conversation of his friends; and, sometimes in the evening, with a party at his favourite game of whist. His cheerfulness was so great, and his conversation and amusements run so much in their usual strain, that, notwithstanding all bad symptoms, many people could not believe he was dying. "I shall tell your friend, Colonel Edmondstone," said Doctor Dundas to him one day, "that I left you much better, and in a fair way of recovery."[4] "Doctor," said he, "as I believe you would not chuse to tell any thing but the truth, you had better tell him, that I am dying as fast as my enemies, if I have any, could wish, and as easily and cheerfully as my best friends could desire."[5] Colonel Edmondstone soon afterwards came to see him, and take leave of him; and on his way home, he could not forbear writing him a letter bidding him once more an eternal adieu, and applying to him, as to a dying man, the beautiful French verses in which the Abbé Chaulieu, in expectation of his own death, laments his approaching separation from his friend, the Marquis de la Fare.[6] Mr. Hume's magnanimity and

3. Home kept a diary of the first part of this trip that includes running commentary on Hume's activities, health, and spirits: see ibid., 168–82.

4. James Edmonstoune of Newton, a longtime military officer, was an old friend of Hume's; he was part of the expedition to the coast of France in 1746 under Lieutenant-General James St. Clair (see p. 37 in this volume). The "Doctor Dundas" mentioned here has not been traced.

5. The phrase "if I have any" was inserted at the suggestion of Hume's brother: see John Home of Ninewells to Adam Smith, 14 October 1776, in CAS, 215.

6. For Edmonstoune's letter and the verses from the abbé Chaulieu, see pp. 53–54 in this volume.

firmness were such, that his most affectionate friends knew, that they hazarded nothing in talking or writing to him as to a dying man, and that so far from being hurt by this frankness, he was rather pleased and flattered by it. I happened to come into his room while he was reading this letter, which he had just received, and which he immediately showed me.[7] I told him, that though I was sensible how very much he was weakened, and that appearances were in many respects very bad, yet his cheerfulness was still so great, the spirit of life seemed still to be so very strong in him, that I could not help entertaining some faint hopes. He answered, "Your hopes are groundless. An habitual diarrhœa of more than a year's standing, would be a very bad disease at any age: at my age it is a mortal one. When I lie down in the evening, I feel myself weaker than when I rose in the morning; and when I rise in the morning, weaker than when I lay down in the evening. I am sensible, besides, that some of my vital parts are affected, so that I must soon die." "Well," said I, "if it must be so, you have at least the satisfaction of leaving all your friends, your brother's family in particular, in great prosperity." He said that he felt that satisfaction so sensibly, that when he was reading a few days before, Lucian's Dialogues of the Dead, among all the excuses which are alleged to Charon for not entering readily into his boat, he could not find one that fitted him; he had no house to finish, he had no daughter to provide for, he had no enemies upon whom he wished to revenge himself.[8] "I could not well imagine,"

---

7. Smith was living with Hume at the time; he stayed at Hume's house in the New Town for most of the period from Hume's return to Edinburgh on July 3 through mid-August. See David Hume to John Home of Ninewells, 25 July 1776, in Sadao Ikeda, *David Hume and the Eighteenth Century British Thought: An Annotated Catalogue* (Tokyo: Chuo University Library, 1986), 219. For an earlier account of the conversation that follows, see pp. 55–56 in this volume.

8. Charon is, in Greek mythology, the boatman who carries the souls of the recently deceased across the River Styx into Hades. Judging from Smith's description, the work that Hume was reading was probably Lucian's *The Downward Journey* rather than the *Dialogues of the Dead*. For discussion, see Annette C. Baier, "Hume's Deathbed Reading: A Tale of Three Letters," in *Death and Character: Further Reflections on Hume* (Cambridge, MA: Harvard University Press, 2008), 100–110. William Cullen's account of this conversation has Hume reading "the dialogue entitled Kataplous"—the Greek title of *The Downward Journey*. See William Cullen to John Hunter, 17 September 1776, in John Thomson, *An Account of the Life, Lectures, and Writings of William Cullen, M. D.*, vol. 1 (Edinburgh: William Blackwood, 1832), 608. Lucian was a scourge of superstition and a favorite of both Hume and Smith. One of Hume's correspondents in fact suggests that Lucian was his "favorite author": see the abbé Morellet to David Hume, 8 September 1766, in HL II, 157–58 n. 1. Smith, for his part, proclaimed to his students that "in a word there is no author from whom more reall instruction and good sense can be found than Lucian." Just over a week later he informed them that Lucian's "design" was "to overthrow

said he, "what excuse I could make to Charon in order to obtain a little delay. I have done every thing of consequence which I ever meant to do, and I could at no time expect to leave my relations and friends in a better situation than that in which I am now likely to leave them; I, therefore, have all reason to die contented." He then diverted himself with inventing several jocular excuses, which he supposed he might make to Charon, and with imagining the very surly answers which it might suit the character of Charon to return to them. "Upon further consideration," said he, "I thought I might say to him, Good Charon, I have been correcting my works for a new edition. Allow me a little time, that I may see how the Public receives the alterations." But Charon would answer, "When you have seen the effect of these, you will be for making other alterations. There will be no end of such excuses; so, honest friend, please step into the boat." But I might still urge, "Have a little patience, good Charon, I have been endeavouring to open the eyes of the Public. If I live a few years longer, I may have the satisfaction of seeing the downfal of some of the prevailing systems of superstition."[9] But Charon would then lose all temper and decency. "You loitering rogue, that will not happen these many hundred years. Do you fancy I will grant you a lease for so long a term? Get into the boat this instant, you lazy loitering rogue."

But, though Mr. Hume always talked of his approaching dissolution with great cheerfulness, he never affected to make any parade of his magnanimity. He never mentioned the subject but when the conversation naturally led to it, and never dwelt longer upon it than the course of the conversation happened to require: it was a subject indeed which occurred pretty frequently, in consequence of the inquiries which his friends, who came to see him, naturally made concerning the state of his health. The

---

the present fabric of Theology and Philosophy" without, however, having any "design of erecting an other in its place." Adam Smith, *Lectures on Rhetoric and Belles Lettres*, ed. J. C. Bryce (Indianapolis: Liberty Fund, [1762–1763] 1985), 51, 60; see also 49–50.

9. Smith's account of this conversation in his letter to Alexander Wedderburn has Hume hoping for "the pleasure of seeing the churches shut up, and the Clergy sent about their business": see p. 56 in this volume. In William Cullen's version of the conversation, apparently related secondhand from Smith, Hume claims that he is "busily employed in making his countrymen wiser, and particularly in delivering them from the Christian superstition." William Cullen to John Hunter, 17 September 1776, in Thomson, *An Account of the Life, Lectures, and Writings of William Cullen*, 608. Note that the editor of Cullen's writings, John Thomson, omits the words "the Christian" in his transcription: see Ernest Campbell Mossner, *The Life of David Hume*, second edition (Oxford: Clarendon Press, 1980), 601 n. 1.

conversation which I mentioned above, and which passed on Thursday the 8th of August, was the last, except one, that I ever had with him. He had now become so very weak, that the company of his most intimate friends fatigued him; for his cheerfulness was still so great, his complaisance and social disposition were still so entire, that when any friend was with him, he could not help talking more, and with greater exertion, than suited the weakness of his body. At his own desire, therefore, I agreed to leave Edinburgh, where I was staying partly upon his account, and returned to my mother's house here, at Kirkaldy, upon condition that he would send for me whenever he wished to see me; the physician who saw him most frequently, Doctor Black, undertaking, in the mean time, to write me occasionally an account of the state of his health.[10]

On the 22nd of August, the Doctor wrote me the following letter:

"Since my last, Mr. Hume has passed his time pretty easily, but is much weaker. He sits up, goes down stairs once a day, and amuses himself with reading, but seldom sees any body. He finds that even the conversation of his most intimate friends fatigues and oppresses him; and it is happy that he does not need it, for he is quite free from anxiety, impatience, or low spirits, and passes his time very well with the assistance of amusing books."[11]

I received the day after a letter from Mr. Hume himself, of which the following is an extract.

Edinburgh, 23d August, 1776.

"MY DEAREST FRIEND,

I am obliged to make use of my nephew's hand in writing to you, as I do not rise today.

I go very fast to decline, and last night had a small fever, which I hoped might put a quicker period to this tedious illness, but unluckily it has, in

10. In addition to being a physician, Joseph Black (1728–1799) was an eminent chemist and a former colleague of Smith's at Glasgow University. Black and Smith, along with the geologist James Hutton (1726–1797), would later form a weekly dining group in Edinburgh called the Oyster Club (also sometimes known as Adam Smith's Club). Black and Hutton would also be Smith's literary executors. For Black's updates on Hume's health, see Joseph Black to Adam Smith, 14 August 1776, in CAS, 204–5; and Joseph Black to Adam Smith, 22 August 1776, in CAS, 207.

11. Smith omits the first and last sentences of the letter. For the full letter, see Joseph Black to Adam Smith, 22 August 1776, in CAS, 207.

a great measure, gone off. I cannot submit to your coming over here on my account, as it is possible for me to see you so small a part of the day, but Doctor Black can better inform you concerning the degree of strength which may from time to time remain with me. Adieu, & c."[12]

Three days after I received the following letter from Doctor Black.

Edinburgh, Monday, 26th August, 1776.

"DEAR SIR,

Yesterday about four o'clock afternoon, Mr. Hume expired. The near approach of his death became evident in the night between Thursday and Friday, when his disease became excessive, and soon weakened him so much, that he could no longer rise out of his bed. He continued to the last perfectly sensible, and free from much pain or feelings of distress. He never dropped the smallest expression of impatience; but when he had occasion to speak to the people about him, always did it with affection and tenderness. I thought it improper to write to bring you over, especially as I heard that he had dictated a letter to you desiring you not to come. When he became very weak, it cost him an effort to speak, and he died in such a happy composure of mind, that nothing could exceed it."[13]

Thus died our most excellent, and never to be forgotten friend[14]; concerning whose philosophical opinions men will, no doubt, judge variously, every one approving, or condemning them, according as they happen to coincide or disagree with his own; but concerning whose character and conduct there can scarce be a difference of opinion. His temper, indeed,

---

12. Smith omits two paragraphs after the opening sentence, the first relating to the publication of Hume's *Dialogues Concerning Natural Religion* and the second granting Smith "entire liberty to make what Additions you please to the account of my Life." Smith also omits a postscript. For the full letter, see David Hume to Adam Smith, 23 August 1776, in HL II, 335–36, and CAS, 208.

13. Smith tones down some of the more graphic details of the original letter. For instance, whereas Black wrote that in the night between Thursday and Friday "the looseness became very excessive and was attended with vomiting now and then," Smith has him say simply that "his disease became excessive." He also slightly alters the end of the final sentence: Black wrote that Hume "died in such a happy composure of mind that nothing could have made it better." For the full letter, see Joseph Black to Adam Smith, 26 August 1776, in CAS, 208–9.

14. In a letter to Hume's brother Smith similarly refers to Hume as "your never to be forgotten brother": see Adam Smith to John Home of Ninewells, 7 October 1776, in CAS, 214. Smith later applied the epithet "never to be forgotten" to his teacher, Francis Hutcheson: see Adam Smith to Archibald Davidson, 16 November 1787, in CAS, 309.

seemed to be more happily balanced, if I may be allowed such an expression, than that perhaps of any other man I have ever known. Even in the lowest state of his fortune, his great and necessary frugality never hindered him from exercising, upon proper occasions, acts both of charity and generosity. It was a frugality founded, not upon avarice, but upon the love of independency. The extreme gentleness of his nature never weakened either the firmness of his mind, or the steadiness of his resolutions. His constant pleasantry was the genuine effusion of good-nature and good-humour, tempered with delicacy and modesty, and without even the slightest tincture of malignity, so frequently the disagreeable source of what is called wit in other men. It never was the meaning of his raillery to mortify; and therefore, far from offending, it seldom failed to please and delight, even those who were the objects of it. To his friends, who were frequently the objects of it, there was not perhaps any one of all his great and amiable qualities, which contributed more to endear his conversation. And that gaiety of temper, so agreeable in society, but which is so often accompanied with frivolous and superficial qualities, was in him certainly attended with the most severe application, the most extensive learning, the greatest depth of thought, and a capacity in every respect the most comprehensive.[15] Upon the whole, I have always considered him, both in his lifetime and since his death, as approaching as nearly to the idea of a perfectly wise and virtuous man, as perhaps the nature human frailty will permit.[16]

I ever am, dear Sir,
Most affectionately your's,
ADAM SMITH.

---

15. Andrew Corsa has called attention to the many similarities between Smith's description of Hume in this paragraph and Hume's own description of the "model of perfect virtue," Cleanthes, in his *Second Enquiry*. See David Hume, *An Enquiry Concerning the Principles of Morals*, ed. Tom L. Beauchamp (Oxford: Clarendon Press, [1751] 1998), 9.2, 72–73; and Andrew Corsa, "Modern Greatness of Soul in Hume and Smith," *Ergo, an Open Access Journal of Philosophy* 2.2 (2015), 48–49.

16. There is a clear echo here of Plato's epitaph for Socrates in the concluding sentence of the *Phaedo*, in which the narrator, Phaedo, pronounces Socrates to be "of all those whom we knew in our time, the bravest and also the wisest and most upright." Plato, *Phaedo*, in *The Collected Dialogues of Plato*, ed. Edith Hamilton and Huntington Cairns (Princeton: Princeton University Press, 1961), 98.

# James Edmonstoune to David Hume, 7 August 1776

To David Hume Esq
No. 10. Newtown
Edinburgh

Linlithgow
Wedensday.

My Dear Dear David

My Heart is very full. I could not see you this Morning.[1] I thought it was better for us both. You can't die, you must live in the Memory of all your Friends and Acquaintances and your Works will render you immortal. I could never conceive that it was possible for any one to dislike you or hate you, he must be more than savage who could be an Enemy to a Man of the best Head and Heart and of the most amiable Manners.

O Toi qui de mon Ame
Est la chere Moitie
Toi qui joins la delicatesse
Des Sentimens d'une Maitresse
A la Solidité d'une sure Amitié
David, il faut bientot que le Parque cruelle

1. As Smith notes in the *Letter to Strahan* (see p. 46 in this volume), Edmonstoune had just visited the ailing Hume in Edinburgh and wrote this letter on the way home to bid him a final adieu.

Vienne rompre des si beaux Noeuds
& malgré nos Cris & nos Vœux
Bientot nous essuyerons une absence eternelle.[2] Adieu Adieu

J. E.

What I mention'd to you about Hume Castle in Joke I now intend in Earnest.[3] I shall dedicate it to you and Baron Mure[4]; I want an Inscription. I wish you would cause some of your Friends to compose a short one once more Adieu

---

2. As Smith notes in the *Letter to Strahan* (see p. 46 in this volume), these verses were composed by Guillaume Amfrye de Chaulieu (1639–1720), a French poet, about his close friend, Charles Auguste, Marquis de la Fare (1644–1712), another French poet. Though Chaulieu wrote the "Épître à M. le Marquis de la Fare qui m'avait demandé mon Portrait" (1703) in anticipation of his own death, in fact he did not die for another seventeen years. Edmonstoune reproduces the first eight lines of the 217-line poem, splitting the first line in two and substituting "David" for "La Fare" in the fifth line. I have preserved Edmonstoune's spelling and accents, which differ in a number of instances from the original text. Though translating poetry is notoriously difficult, a literal rendering would look something like this:

O You who of my Soul
Are the better Half
You who join the delicacy
Of the Sentiments of a Mistress
To the Solidity of a steady Friendship
David, it must be soon that cruel Fate
Will come to break such beautiful Knots
And despite our Cries and our Wishes
Soon we will suffer an eternal absence.

3. Hume Castle was built in the thirteenth century in Berwickshire, near the border with England. It stood around fifteen miles from Hume's childhood home at Ninewells, though it had been reduced to ruins by Oliver Cromwell's army in 1651. In the early 1770s the site was purchased by Hugh Hume-Campbell, 3rd Earl of Marchmont (1708–1794), who rebuilt the castle as a sort of folly. There is no record of the castle having been dedicated in the manner that Edmonstoune describes.

4. William Mure of Caldwell (1718–1776) was a longtime Member of Parliament, baron of the Scots exchequer, and one of Hume's oldest and closest friends. He had died less than five months earlier, on 25 March 1776.

# Adam Smith to Alexander Wedderburn, 14 August 1776

To Alexander Wedderburne
Esquire, M. P.
Lincolns Inn Fields
London

My Dear Sir

It gives me very great concern to learn by Mr Cunningham that Mrs Wedderburnes state of Health obliges you to pass some months at Spaw.[1] I would hope, however, that necessity is only the pretence and that amusement is the real purpose of your journey, which will at any rate remove you from a scene of Business and anxiety to one of Pleasure and dissipation.

I have nothing to tell you that will be very agreable. Poor David Hume is dying very fast, but with great chearfulness and good humour and with more real resignation to the necessary course of things, than any whining Christian ever dyed with pretended resignation to the will of God.[2] On thursday last he showed me a letter from his old friend Collonel Edmondstone bidding him an eternal adieu.[3] I alledged that as his spirits were so

1. This is presumably a reference to the spa at Harrogate in North Yorkshire, where Wedderburn had recently acquired property. The "Mr Cunningham" mentioned here has not been traced.

2. Smith seems to have reserved the word "whining" for references to Christians and Christian-inspired ideas: see also Adam Smith, *The Theory of Moral Sentiments*, ed. D. D. Raphael and A. L. Macfie (Indianapolis: Liberty Fund, [1759–90] 1982), III.3.8, 139; and VII.ii.1.29, 283. In both cases, the term was added in the sixth edition of 1790.

3. See pp. 53–54 in this volume.

very good there was still some chance that his disease might take a favourable turn. He answered, 'Smith, your hopes are groundless; an habitual diarrhœa, which has now continued for several years, is a dangerous disease to a man of any age. At my age it is a mortal one. When I rise in the morning I find myself weaker than when I went to bed at night, and when I go to bed at night weaker than when I rose in the morning, so that in a few days I trust the business will be over.' I said, that at any rate he had the comfort of thinking that he left all his friends in prosperity particularly his brothers family whose circumstances would be greatly improved by his means. He replied, their circumstances were good independent of me and gave me some account of them: but, continued he, I so far agree with you, that when I was lately reading the dialogues of Lucian in which he represents one Ghost as pleading for a short delay till he should marry a young daughter, another till he should finish a house he had begun, a third till he had provided a portion for two or three young Children, I began to think of what Excuse I could alledge to Charon in order to procure a short delay, and as I have now done every thing that I ever intended to do, I acknowledge that for some time no tolerable one occurred to me; at last I thought I might say, Good Charon, I have been endeavouring to open the eyes of the people; have a little patience only till I have the pleasure of seeing the churches shut up, and the Clergy sent about their business[4]; but Charon would reply, O you loitering rogue; that wont happen these two hundred years; do you fancy I will give you a lease for so long a time? Get into the boat this instant. Since we must lose our friend the most agreable thing that can happen is that he dyes as a man of sense ought to do. I left Edinburgh for a few days till he should recall me. He is so weak, that even my company fatigues him, especially as his spirits are so good that he cannot help talking incessantly when anybody is with him. When alone

4. There is an echo here of a recently discovered letter of the previous year in which Hume expresses his desire to see "all the Churches . . . converted into Riding Schools, Manufactories, Tennis Courts or Playhouses." In this letter, however, he says—surely jokingly—that he expects to see this objective "much advanced" within his own lifetime. David Hume to Andrew Stuart of Torrance, 1 August 1775, in Maurice Baumstark, "The End of Empire and the Death of Religion: A Reconsideration of Hume's Later Political Thought," in *Philosophy and Religion in Enlightenment Britain*, ed. Ruth Savage (Oxford: Oxford University Press, 2012), 257.

he diverts himself with [][5] with correcting his own works, and with all [] ordinary amusements.

I do not very well remember what were the [] books I recommended to Sir James Erskine.[6] The [] *des Etudes du duc de Parme*[7] was probably [] them. I cannot guess at the other.

Is McDonald[8] of your Party? His health, I hear, is not good. I should be much obliged to you for an account of it. After Hume there is scarce anybody I would more sincerely regret. I ever am

My Dear Sir
Yours entirely
Adam Smith

Kirkaldy
Fifeshire
14 august 1776.

---

5. The manuscript is torn slightly here; this and the following sets of square brackets indicate where a word may be missing.

6. Sir James Erskine, later General James St. Claire-Erskine, 2nd Earl of Rosslyn (1762–1837), was Wedderburn's young nephew, then studying at Eton. Erskine's father had died in 1765, and Wedderburn took on the responsibility of overseeing his education. Smith is here responding to a query in Wedderburn's previous letter: "I remember you mentioned two Books to me that would be of service to Sir James Erskine, and I have forgot the titles of them. If they occurr to you, I should be very glad to have them, as I must in a few weeks find some employment for his Curiosity." Alexander Wedderburn to Adam Smith, 6 June 1776, in CAS, 198.

7. Étienne Bonnot de Condillac's massive *Cours d'études pour l'instruction du prince de Parme* (1775) was composed in the process of tutoring Duke Ferdinand of Parma, Louis XV's grandson.

8. The editors of CAS plausibly suggest that this is a reference to Archibald Macdonald (1747–1826), a rising lawyer at Lincoln's Inn: see 204 n. 6.

# A Letter to Adam Smith LL.D. on the Life, Death, and Philosophy of His Friend David Hume Esq.

## *By One of the People Called Christians*

George Horne

*Ibant obscuri, solâ sub nocte, per umbram,*
*Perque domos Ditis vacuas, et inania regna.*

VIRG.[1]

### ADVERTISEMENT

It is of no consequence, gentle Reader, to you, any more than it is to Dr. SMITH, that you should know the name of the person, who now addresseth you.[2] Your mind cannot be biassed, either way, by that, of which you remain ignorant. The remarks in the following pages are not therefore true, or false, because I made them; but I made them, because I thought them to be true. Read, consider, and determine for yourself. If you find no satisfaction, throw the book into the fire, regret (but with moderation, as becometh a philosopher) the loss of your shilling; and take care not to lose another, in the same manner. If, on the contrary, you *should* find satisfaction (and, it is humbly hoped, you will find a great deal) neglect not to communicate to others, what has thus been communicated to you. Speak handsomely of me, wherever you go, and introduce me to your

1. "On they went, those dim travelers under the lonely night, through the gloom and the empty halls of Death's ghostly realm." Virgil, *The Aeneid*, trans. Robert Fagles (New York: Penguin, 2006), 191.

2. In the 1799 edition, the first to appear after Horne's death, the following note was included immediately after the title page: "N. B. *The Author of this Tract was GEORGE HORNE, D.D. Late Lord Bishop of Norwich.*"

kinsfolk and acquaintance. The enemies of Religion are awake; let not her friends sleep.

I intended a much longer work; but, like the learned editor of Mr. HUME's Life, am necessitated to "gratify," with all possible expedition, "the impatience of the public curiosity"[3]; so eager is it to hear, what they, who believe in GOD, can possibly have to say for themselves. And if this will do the business, why should you be troubled with more? I am far from agreeing with Mr. VOLTAIRE, in all his observations. But there is one, in which it is impossible to disagree with him. "I have said, and I abide by it," cries the little hero, "that the fault of most books is, their being too large."[4] On reviewing what I have written, I really cannot see there is occasion to add another sentence.

Had I not chosen, for reasons best known to myself, thus to make my appearance *incog.* I would certainly have sate for my picture, and have tried to cast a look at my title page, as lively and good humoured, as that of Mr. HUME himself. My bookseller, indeed, told me, it would have been a much more creditable way of doing the thing; "and then, you know, Sir," said he, "we could have charged the other sixpence."[5]

## A
## LETTER, &C.

SIR,

You have been lately employed in embalming a philosopher; his *body*, I believe I must say; for concerning the other part of him, neither you nor he seem to have entertained an idea, sleeping or waking. Else, it surely might have claimed a little of your care and attention; and one would think, the belief of the soul's existence and immortality could do no harm,

---

3. See the introduction to this volume, p. 18. The "learned editor" is, of course, William Strahan.

4. Horne seems to have taken this quotation from a letter from Voltaire to the Dutch mathematician Willem 's Gravesande (1688–1742) of 1 June 1741, published as "A Letter from the Author to Mr. S. Gravesand, Professor of Mathematics," in *The Works of M. de Voltaire*, trans. Tobias Smollett, vol. 18 (London: J. Newbery et al., 1762), 223.

5. Whereas Horne's *Letter* was priced at one shilling, as noted in the first paragraph of the advertisement, Strahan's edition of *The Life of David Hume* included an engraved portrait of Hume as a frontispiece and cost one shilling, six pence.

if it did no good, in a *Theory of Moral Sentiments*. But every gentleman understands his own business best.

Will you do an unknown correspondent the honour, Sir, to accept a few plain remarks, in a free and easy way, upon the curious letter to Mr. STRAHAN, in which this ever memorable operation of *embalming* is performed? Our Philosopher's account of *his own life* will likewise be considered, as we go along.

Trust me, good Doctor, I am no bigot, enthusiast, or enemy to human learning—*Et ego in Arcadiâ*[6]—I have made many a hearty meal, in private, upon CICERO and VIRGIL, as well as Mr. HUME.[a] Few persons (though, perhaps, as Mr. HUME says, upon a like occasion, "I ought not to judge on that subject"[7]) have a quicker relish for the productions of genius, and the beauties of composition. It is therefore as little in my intention, as it is in my power, to prejudice the literary character of your friend. From some of his writings I have received great pleasure, and have ever esteemed his History of England to have been a noble effort of *Matter and Motion*. But when a man takes it into his head to do mischief, you must be sensible, Sir, the Public has always reason to lament his being *a clever fellow*.

I hope it will not be deemed vanity in me likewise to say, that I have in my composition a large proportion of that, which our inimitable SHAKESPEARE styles, *the milk of human kindness*.[8] I never knew what envy or hatred was; and am ready, at all times, to praise, wherever I can do it, in honour and conscience. DAVID, I doubt not, was, as you affirm, a social agreeable person, of a convivial turn, told a good story, and played well at "his favourite game of whist."[b] I know not that JOHN THE PAINTER[9]

---

6. Usually rendered as "Et in Arcadia ego," this phrase can be translated as "Even in Arcadia, there am I" or "I too live(d) in Arcadia." Arcadia was a region in the central Peloponnese that was often depicted as a pastoral paradise. The phrase has a long and complicated history in both painting and print: see Erwin Panofsky, "Et in Arcadia Ego," in *Philosophy & History: Essays Presented to Ernst Cassirer*, ed. Raymond Klibansky and H. J. Paton (Oxford: Clarendon Press, 1936).

a. LIFE, p. 5. [Lettered footnotes are Horne's; numbered footnotes and material in square brackets have been added by the present editor. Horne's reference here corresponds to p. 36 in this volume.]

7. See p. 39 in this volume.

8. See William Shakespeare, *Macbeth*, Act 1, scene 5.

b. LIFE, &c. p. 43. [See p. 46 in this volume.]

9. James Aitkin (1752–1777), aka "John the Painter," was a disaffected Scot who, as Horne goes on to note, attempted to burn down the Royal Navy's dockyards in several cities

did the same. But there is no absurdity in the supposition. If he did not, he might have done it—Doctor, be not offended—I mean no harm. I would only infer thus much, that I could not, on that account, bring myself absolutely to approve his odd fancy of firing all the dockyards in the kingdom.

Concerning the *philosophical opinions* of Mr. HUME you observe,[c] that "men will, no doubt, judge variously." They are certainly at liberty so to do, because the author himself did the same. Sometimes, to be sure, he esteemed them ingenious, deep, subtle, elegant, and calculated to diffuse his literary fame to the ends of the world. But, at other times, he judged very differently; very much so, indeed. "I dine, says he, I play a game at back-gammon, I converse, and am merry with my friends; and when, after three or four hours amusement, I would return to these speculations, they appear so *cold*, so *strained*, and so *ridiculous*, that I cannot find in my heart to enter into them any farther.[d] Now, Sir, if you will only give me leave to judge, before dinner, of Mr. HUME's philosophy, as he judged of it after dinner, we shall have no farther dispute upon that subject. Only I could wish, if it were possible, to have a scheme of thought, which would bear contemplating, at any time of the day; because, otherwise, a person must be at the expence of maintaining a brace of these metaphysical Hobby-Horses, one to mount in the morning, and the other in the afternoon.

After all, Sir, friend as I am to freedom of opinion (and no one living can be more so) I am rather sorry, methinks, that men should judge so *variously* of Mr. HUME's philosophical speculations. For since the design of them is to banish out of the world every idea of truth and comfort, salvation and immortality, a future state, and the providence, and even

---

in southern England as an act of terror in 1776–1777. He was executed on 10 March 1777, the day before Strahan released *The Life of David Hume*.

c. LIFE, &c. p. 59. [See p. 50 in this volume.]

d. *Treatise of Human Nature*. I. 467. In the Postscript to this Letter, a view will be given of the HUMIAN system, taken exactly as it appeared to it's author at six o'clock in the evening. [Horne's reference is to the famous conclusion of Book 1 of Hume's *Treatise*: see David Hume, *A Treatise of Human Nature*, ed. David Fate Norton and Mary J. Norton (Oxford: Clarendon Press, [1739–1740] 2007), 1.4.7.9, 175. The context should be consulted: the "speculations" that Hume finds cold, strained, and ridiculous after a few hours of amusement are not his own "philosophical opinions," as Horne suggests, but rather certain extreme skeptical views. The quoted passage is part of a sort of a dialectic that concludes with Hume adopting not extreme skepticism but rather what he would later call "*mitigated* scepticism." See David Hume, *An Enquiry Concerning Human Understanding*, ed. Tom L. Beauchamp (Oxford: Clarendon Press, [1748] 2000), 12.24–5, 120–21.]

existence of GOD, it seems a pity, that we cannot be all of a mind about them, though we might have formerly liked to hear the author crack a joke, over a bottle, in his life time. And I could have been well pleased to have been informed by you, Sir, that, before his death, he had ceased to number among his happy effusions tracts of this kind and tendency.

For—(let me come a little closer to you, Doctor, if you please, upon this subject—Don't be under any apprehensions—my name does not begin with a B–[10]) Are *you* sure, and can you make *us* sure, that there really exist no such things as a GOD, and a future state of rewards and punishments? If so, all is well. Let us *then*, in our last hours, read LUCIAN, and play at WHIST, and droll upon CHARON and his boat[e]; let us die as foolish and insensible, as much like our brother philosophers, the calves of the field, and the asses of the desart, as we can, for the life of us. But—if such things BE—as they most certainly ARE—Is it right in you, Sir, to hold up to our view, as "perfectly wise and virtuous,"[f] the *character* and *conduct* of one, who seems to have been possessed with an incurable antipathy to all that is called RELIGION; and who strained every nerve to explode, suppress, and extirpate the spirit of it among men, that it's very name, if he could effect it, might no more be had in remembrance? Are we, do you imagine, to be reconciled to a character of this sort, and fall in love with it, because it's owner was *good company*, and knew how to manage his *cards*? Low as the age is fallen, I will venture to hope, it has grace enough yet left, to resent such usage as this.

You endeavour to entertain us with some *pleasant conceits* that were supposed by Mr. HUME to pass between himself and old CHARON. The philosopher tells the old gentleman, that "he had been endeavouring to open the eyes of the Public"; that he was "correcting his works for a new edition," from which great things were to be expected; in short, "if he could but live a few years longer (and that was the only reason why he would wish to do so) he might have the satisfaction of seeing the downfal of some of the prevailing systems of *superstition*."[g]

---

10. James Beattie (1735–1803) was a proponent of the Scottish "common sense" philosophy and one of Hume's harshest and most prominent critics. See also footnote 12 below.

e. LIFE, &c. p. 47, et seq. [See pp. 47–48 in this volume.]

f. LIFE, &c. p. 62. [See p. 51 in this volume.]

g. LIFE, &c. p. 50. [See p. 48 in this volume.]

We all know, Sir, what the word SUPERSTITION denotes, in Mr. HUME's vocabulary, and against what Religion his shafts are levelled, under that name. But, Doctor SMITH, do you believe, or would you have us to believe, that it is CHARON, who calls us out of the world, at the appointed time? Doth not HE call us out of it, who sent us into it? Let me, then, present you with a paraphrase of the Wish, as addressed to HIM, to whom it should, and to whom alone, with any sense and propriety, it can be addressed.—Thus it runs—

"LORD, I have only one reason why I would wish to live. Suffer me so to do, I most humbly beseech thee, yet a little while, till mine eyes shall behold the success of my undertaking to overthrow, by my metaphysics, the faith which thy SON descended from heaven to plant, and to root out the knowledge and the love of thee from the earth."

Here are no rhetorical figures, no hyperbole's, or exaggerations. The matter is even so. I appeal, in the face of the world, Sir, to yourself, and to every man, who can read and understand the writings of Mr. HUME, whether this be not, in plain, honest English, the drift of his *philosophy*, as it is called; for the propagation of which alone he wished to live; and concerning which you are pleased to say coolly, "men will judge variously, every one approving or condemning these opinions, according as they happen to coincide or disagree with his own."[h] Our thoughts are very naturally carried back, upon this occasion, to the author of the *first philosophy*, who likewise engaged to *open the eyes of the Public*—He did so; but the only discovery they found themselves able to make, was,—that they were NAKED.

You talk much, Sir, of our philosopher's *gentleness* of manners, *good nature*, *compassion*, *generosity*, *charity*. Alas, Sir, whither were they all fled, when he so often sate down calmly and deliberately to obliterate from the hearts of the human species every trace of the knowledge of GOD and his dispensations; all faith in his kind providence, and fatherly protection; all hope of enjoying his grace and favour, here, or hereafter; all love of him, and of their brethren for his sake; all the patience under tribulation, all the comforts, in time of sorrow, derived from these fruitful and perennial sources? Did a good man think himself able, by the force of metaphysic incantation, in a moment, to blot the sun out of heaven, and

h. LIFE, &c. p. 59. [See p. 50 in this volume.]

dry up every fountain upon earth, would he attempt to do it?—TULLY had but a faint glimpse of the country towards which we are all travelling; yet, so pleasing was any the most imperfect and shadowy prospect into futurity, that TULLY declared, no man should ravish it from him.[i] And surely, TULLY was a philosopher, as well as HUME. O had he seen the light which shone upon HUME, he would not have closed his eyes against it; had the same cup been offered to him, he would not have dashed it untasted from him!

"Perhaps our modern sceptics are ignorant, that without the belief of a GOD, and the hope of immortality, the miseries of human life would often be insupportable. But can I suppose them in a state of total and invincible stupidity, utter strangers to the human heart, and to human affairs? Sure, they would not thank me for such a supposition. Yet this I must suppose, or I must believe them to be the most cruel, the most perfidious, and the most profligate of men. Caressed by those who call themselves the great, ingrossed by the formalities of life, intoxicated with vanity, pampered with adulation, dissipated in the tumult of business, or amidst the vicissitudes of folly, they perhaps have little need and little relish for the consolations of religion. But let them know, that in the solitary scenes of life, there is many an honest and tender heart pining with incurable anguish, pierced with the sharpest sting of disappointment, bereft of friends, chilled with poverty, racked with disease, scourged by the oppressor; whom nothing but trust in Providence, and the hope of a future retribution could preserve from the agonies of despair. And do they, with sacrilegious hands, attempt to violate this last refuge of the miserable, and to rob them of the only comfort that had survived the ravages of misfortune, malice, and tyranny? Did it ever happen, that the influence of their execrable tenets disturbed the tranquillity of virtuous retirement, deepened the gloom of human distress, or aggravated the horrors of the grave? Is it possible, that this may have happened in many instances? Is it probable, that this hath happened in one single instance?—Ye traitors to human kind, ye murderers of the

i. Quod si in hoc erro, quod animos hominum immortales esse credam, libenter erro; nec mihi hunc errorem, quo delector, dum vivo, extorqueri volo. DE SENECTUTE, ad Fin. ["And if I err in my belief that the souls of men are immortal, I gladly err, nor do I wish this error which gives me pleasure to be wrested from me while I live." Cicero, *De Senectute*, in *On Old Age, On Friendship, On Divination*, trans. W. A. Falconer (Cambridge, MA: Harvard University Press, 1923), 96–97.]

human soul, how can ye answer for it to your own hearts! Surely, every spark of your generosity is extinguished for ever, if this consideration do not awaken in you the keenest remorse, and make you wish in bitterness of soul—But I remonstrate in vain. All this must have often occurred to you, and been as often rejected, as utterly frivolous. Could I enforce the present topic by an appeal to your vanity, I might possibly make some impression. But to plead with you on the principles of BENEVOLENCE, or GENEROSITY, is to address you in a language ye do not, or will not, understand; and as to the shame of being convicted of absurdity, ignorance, or want of candour, ye have long ago proved yourselves superior to the sense of it.—But let not the lovers of truth be discouraged. Atheism cannot be of long continuance, nor is there much danger of it's becoming universal. The influence of some conspicuous characters hath brought it too much into fashion; which, in a thoughtless and profligate age, it is no difficult matter to accomplish. But when men have retrieved the powers of serious reflection, they will find it a frightful phantom; and the mind will return gladly and eagerly to it's old endearments. One thing we certainly know; the fashion of sceptical and metaphysical systems passeth away. Those unnatural productions, the vile effusion of a hard and stupid heart, that mistakes it's own restlessness for the activity of genius, and it's own captiousness for sagacity of understanding, may, like other monsters, please awhile by their singularity; but the charm is soon over; and the succeeding age will be astonished to hear, that their fore-fathers were deluded, or amused, with such fooleries."[11]

You, Sir, have read the preceding paragraph before; but this Letter may come into the hands of many, who have not. It is the alarum bell to the admirers of Mr. HUME; and should be rung in their ears, till succeeded by the last trumpet.

And now, Sir, will you give me leave to ask you a few questions? Why all this hurry and bustle, this eagerness to gratify the pretended "impatience of the Public,"[j] and satisfy it, that our philosopher lived and died perfectly composed and easy? Was there, then, any suspicion,

11. The quotation is from James Beattie, *An Essay on the Immutability of Truth; In Opposition to Sophistry and Scepticism* (Edinburgh: A. Kincaid and J. Bell, 1770), Part 3, chapter 3, 499–502.

j. Preface to LIFE, &c. [See the introduction to this volume, p. 18.]

in SCOTLAND, that he might not, at times, be quite so composed and easy as he should have been? Was there any particular BOOK ever written against him, that shook his system to pieces about his ears, and reduced it to a heap of ruins, the success and eclat of which might be supposed to have hurt his mind, and to have affected his health?[12] Was there any AUTHOR, whose *name* his friends never dared to mention before him, and warned all strangers, that were introduced to him, against doing it, because he never failed, when by accident it was done, to fly out into a transport of passion and swearing?[k] Was it deemed necessary, or expedient, on this account, that he should represent himself, and that you should represent him, to have been perfectly secure of the growth and increase of his philosophic reputation,[13] as if no book had been written, which had impaired it; it having been judged much easier to dissemble the fall of DAGON, than to *set him upon his stumps again*?[14] I am a *South* Briton, and, consequently, not acquainted with what passes so far in the opposite quarter. You, Sir, can inform us how these things are; and likewise, when the great work of *benevolence* and *charity*, of *wisdom* and *virtue*, shall be crowned by the publication of a treatise designed to prove the SOUL'S MORTALITY, and another, to justify and recommend SELF MURDER; for which, without doubt, the present and every future age will bless the name of the *gentle* and *amiable* author.[15]

---

12. The "particular BOOK" is James Beattie's *An Essay on the Nature and Immutability of Truth*, quoted at length two paragraphs prior to this one. Beattie is likewise the "AUTHOR" referred to in the following sentence. Beattie's *Essay* is a passionate—at times abusive—attack on philosophical skepticism, particularly Hume's. Despite (or perhaps because of) the book's vituperative character, it was a great commercial and critical success.

k. "I was a man of mild dispositions, of command of temper, little susceptible of enmity, and of great moderation in all my passions. Even my love of literary fame, my ruling passion, never soured my temper." LIFE, p. 32 [see p. 43 in this volume]. Yet even by what is said of the Reverends and Right Reverends—Bishop WARBURTON, Bishop HURD, the *Zealots* (that is, the *Christians*) and of the resolution once taken to "change his name, and settle in France," because his writings did not meet with sufficient encouragement [see pp. 38, 40, 37, and 40 in this volume, respectively]—by these circumstances, I say, there seems to have been something of the *irritable* in his constitution. But these are trifles. My quarry lies not this way, at present. I fly at nobler game. The atrocious wickedness of diffusing atheism through the land, is a subject which concerns every body.

13. See p. 42 in this volume.

14. See 1 Samuel 5:3–4.

15. Hume had at one point intended to include the essays "Of the Immortality of the Soul" and "Of Suicide" in what became his *Four Dissertations* (1757), but he ended up withdrawing

Upon the whole, Doctor, your meaning is good; but I think you will not succeed, this time. You would persuade us, by the example of DAVID HUME Esq; that atheism is the only cordial for low spirits, and the proper antidote against the fear of death. But, surely, he who can reflect, with complacency, on a friend thus misemploying his talents in his life, and then amusing himself with LUCIAN, WHIST, and CHARON, at his death, may smile over BABYLON in ruins; esteem the earthquake, which destroyed LISBON, an agreeable occurrence; and congratulate the hardened PHARAOH, on his overthrow in the Red sea. Drollery, in such circumstances, is neither more nor less than

Moody Madness, laughing wild,
Amid severest woe.[16]

Would we know the baneful and pestilential influences of false philosophy on the human heart? We need only contemplate them in this most deplorable instance of Mr. HUME.

These sayings, Sir, may appear harsh; but they are salutary. And if departed spirits have any knowledge of what is passing upon earth, that person will be regarded by your friend as rendering him the truest services, who, by energy of expression, and warmth of exhortation, shall most contribute to prevent his writings from producing those effects upon mankind, which he no longer wishes they should produce. Let no man deceive himself, or be deceived by others. It is the voice of eternal TRUTH, which crieth aloud, and saith to you, Sir, and to me, and to all the world—*He that believeth on the Son, hath everlasting life; and he that believeth not the Son, shall not see life; but the wrath of God abideth on him.*[1]

By way of contrast to the behaviour of Mr. HUME, at the close of a life, passed *without* GOD *in the world*, permit me, Sir, to lay before yourself, and the Public, the last sentiments of the truly learned, judicious, and

---

them at the last minute, after copies had already been printed. Some of these copies ended up circulating despite Hume's wishes to the contrary, however, so their existence became a more or less open secret. Unauthorized versions of the two essays were published anonymously in a French translation in 1770 and in English in 1777, and with Hume's name attached in 1783.

16. The quotation is from Thomas Gray's "Ode on a Distant Prospect of Eton College" (1742).

1. JOHN iii.36.

admirable HOOKER, who had spent *his* days in the service of his Maker and Redeemer.[17]

After this manner, therefore, spake the author of the *Ecclesiastical Polity*, immediately before he expired –

"I have lived to see, that this world is made up of perturbations; and I have been long preparing to leave it, and gathering comfort for the dreadful hour of making my account with GOD, which I now apprehend to be near. And though I have, by his grace, loved him in my youth, and feared him in mine age, and laboured to have a conscience void of offence, towards him, and towards all men; yet, if thou, Lord, shouldest be extreme to mark what I have done amiss, who can abide it? And therefore, where I have failed, Lord, shew mercy to me; for I plead not my righteousness, but the forgiveness of my unrighteousness, through His merits, who died to purchase pardon for penitent sinners. And since I owe thee a death, Lord, let it not be terrible, and then take thine own time; I submit to it. Let not mine, O Lord, but thy will be done!—GOD hath heard my daily petitions; for I am at peace with all men, and he is at peace with me. From such blessed assurance I feel that inward joy, which this world can neither give, nor take from me. My conscience beareth me this witness; and this witness makes the thoughts of death joyful. I could wish to live, to do the church more service; but cannot hope it; for my days are past, as a shadow that returns not."[18]

His worthy Biographer adds—"More he would have spoken, but his spirits failed him; and, after a short conflict between nature and death, a quiet sigh put a period to his last breath, and so, he fell asleep—And now he seems to rest like Lazarus in Abraham's bosom.[19] Let me here draw his curtain, till, with the most glorious company of the Patriarchs and Apostles, and the most noble army of Martyrs and Confessors, this most learned, most humble, most holy man shall also awake to receive

---

17. Richard Hooker (1554–1600) was an Anglican priest and one of the most influential theologians of the sixteenth century. His best-known work is *Of the Lawes of Ecclesiastical Politie* (1594).

18. The quotation is from Izaak Walton's "The Life of Mr. Richard Hooker," first published in 1665. See *The Works of That Learned and Judicious Divine Mr. Richard Hooker*, ed. John Keble, seventh edition (Oxford: Clarendon Press, 1888), 85–86.

19. See Luke 16:22.

an eternal tranquility, and with it a greater degree of glory, than common Christians shall be made partakers of."[20]

Doctor SMITH, when the hour of his departure hence shall arrive, will copy the example of the BELIEVER, or the INFIDEL, as it liketh him best. I must freely own, I have no opinion of that reader's *head*, or *heart*, who will not exclaim, as I find myself obliged to do—

*Let* ME *die the death of the Righteous, and let* MY *last end be like his!*[21]

I am, Sir,
Your very sincere
Well-wisher, and
Humble Servant,
One of the People called CHRISTIANS.

## POSTSCRIPT.

As it is possible, Sir, nay, probable, that this little tract, because it is a little one, may be perused by many, who have not leisure or inclination to go through large volumes, and yet wish to know what Mr. HUME's philosophical system is; I shall here subjoin a short, but comprehensive summary of the doctrines which compose it, drawn up, some few years ago, by a learned gentleman, for his amusement, with proper references to those parts of our philosopher's works, where such doctrines were to be found. And though I never heard, the compiler had the thanks of Mr. HUME for so doing, yet neither could I ever find, that he or his friends disputed the fidelity and accuracy with which it was done.[22]

---

20. See Walton, "The Life of Mr. Richard Hooker," in Keble, *The Works of That Learned and Judicious Divine Mr. Richard Hooker*, 86.

21. See Numbers 23:10.

22. Beginning in the fourth edition, published in 1784, the following footnote is included here: "See Dr. BEATTIE's Essay on Truth, Part II. Ch. I. Sect. I, and Part III. Ch. II." Horne's reference corresponds to Beattie, *An Essay on the Immutability of Truth*, 161–72 and 408–84, but the "summary" that follows is culled entirely from pp. 163–66 and 455–57. As a summary of Hume's philosophy it is often inaccurate and never charitable, but correcting each statement would go beyond the scope of these editorial notes.

# A SUMMARY OF MR. HUME'S DOCTRINES, METAPHYSICAL AND MORAL.

## OF THE SOUL.

That the soul of man is not the same this moment, that it was the last; that we know not what it is; that it is not one, but many things; and that it is nothing at all.

That in this soul is the agency of all the causes that operate throughout the sensible creation; and yet that in this soul there is neither power nor agency, nor any idea of either.

That matter and motion may often be regarded as the cause of thought.

## OF THE UNIVERSE.

That the external world does not exist, or at least, that it's existence may reasonably be doubted.

That the universe exists in the mind, and that the mind does not exist.

That the universe is nothing but a heap of perceptions, without a substance.

That though a man could bring himself to believe, yea, and have reason to believe, that every thing in the universe proceeds from some cause; yet it would be unreasonable for him to believe, that the universe itself proceeds from a cause.

## OF HUMAN KNOWLEDGE.

That the perfection of human knowledge is to doubt.

That we ought to doubt of every thing, yea, of our doubts themselves, and therefore, the utmost that philosophy can do, is to give us a doubtful solution of doubtful doubts.[m]

That the human understanding, acting alone, does entirely subvert itself, and prove by argument, that by argument nothing can be proved.

m. The fourth section of Mr. HUME's *Essays om the Human Understanding*, is called, *Sceptical doubts concerning the operations of the human understanding*; and the fifth section bears this title, *Sceptical solution of those doubts*.

That man, in all his perceptions, actions, and volitions, is a mere passive machine, and has no separate existence of his own, being entirely made up of other things, of the existence of which he is by no means certain; and yet, that the nature of all things depends so much upon man, that two and two could not be equal to four, nor fire produce heat, nor the sun light, without an act of the human understanding.

## OF GOD.

That it is unreasonable to believe GOD to be infinitely wise and good, while there is any evil or disorder in the universe.

That we have no good reason to think the universe proceeds from a cause.

That as the existence of the external world is questionable, we are at a loss to find arguments by which we may prove the existence of the Supreme Being, or any of his attributes.

That when we speak of Power, as an attribute of any being, GOD himself not excepted, we use words without meaning.

That we can form no idea of power, nor of any being endued with power, *much less* of one endued with infinite power; and that we can never have reason to believe, that any object, or quality of any object exists, of which we cannot form an idea.[n]

## OF THE MORALITY OF HUMAN ACTIONS.

That every human action is necessary, and could not have been different from what it is.

That moral, intellectual, and corporeal virtues are nearly of the same kind—In other words, that to want honesty, and to want understanding, and to want a leg, are equally the objects of moral disapprobation.

That adultery must be practised, if men would obtain all the advantages of life; that, if generally practised, it would in time cease to be scandalous;

n. The poor prodigal *Gentile*, in the parable, was hardly reduced to feed upon *such* HUSKS as these. How good and how joyful a thing must it be, for one, that has been so reduced, to return to the house of his heavenly Father, where *there is bread enough, and to spare*—to *know the only true* GOD, *and* JESUS CHRIST, *whom he hath sent!* [See Luke 15:16–17.]

and that, if practised secretly and frequently, it would by degrees come to be thought no crime at all.

Lastly, as the soul of man, according to Mr. HUME, becomes every moment a different being, the consequence must be, that the crimes committed by him at one time, cannot be imputable to him at another.[o]

I believe, Doctor SMITH, the reader is now fully prepared to enter into the spirit of your concluding sentence, which therefore shall be mine.

"I have always considered Mr. HUME, both in his lifetime, and since his death, as approaching as nearly to the idea of A PERFECTLY WISE AND VIRTUOUS MAN, as perhaps the nature of human frailty will permit."[23]

THE END.

---

o. "My *Enquiry concerning the Principles of Morals* is of all my writings, historical, philosophical, or literary, incomparably the BEST." LIFE, p. 16. [See p. 39 in this volume.]

23. See p. 51 in this volume.

# Remarks on Dr. Adam Smith's Letter to Mr. Strahan, on the Death of David Hume, Esq.

"E. M."

SIR,

In reading Dr Smith's account of Mr Hume's death, I could not help feeling pain, both for the dead and for his surviving friend, as being one in sentiment, unhappily blind to the "life and immortality brought to light by the gospel."[1]—Doubtless the doctor intends a panegyric upon his friend; but in truth the publication of his frolicsome behaviour in dying, is a satire which must expose Mr H–'s memory to the pity, if not to the contempt, of the truly wise and virtuous part of mankind. It is an affecting picture the doctor exhibits to view. A man of distinguished intellectual powers acting the fool at this end—dying indecently humorous—seemingly easy—"without Christ—without GOD—without hope"[2]—dying in a manner that betrayed a blindness exceeding the darkest ignorance of an *Indian savage.*

From the doctor's narrative of Mr H–'s dying behaviour, a Christian cannot easily allow that the concluding eulogy of his character fairly follows. Can you admit it to be just, to be probable, to be credible, "that such a man approached nearly to the idea of a perfectly wise and virtuous man"?[3] What is this gentleman's notion of wisdom and virtue? If the perfection of impiety, if downright atheism be perfect wisdom and virtue, then it must be granted that his hero was perfectly wise and virtuous. Whether God was at all in Mr H–'s thoughts; or what light God might be pleased to transmit into his mind in his last speechless moments, we

1. See 2 Timothy 1:10.
2. See Ephesians 2:12.
3. See p. 51 in this volume.

know not; but, from the doctor's account, it appears that God was not in any of his words: And was it below the dignity of a philosopher to confess resting on any other prop than his own self-sufficient virtue?—Insolent vanity!

The doctor gives us a sketch of Mr H–'s sublime morals—morals which fitted him to be an agreeable companion to those of his own stamp. Besides his many other amiable qualities, he shone in humorous pleasantry, "without the slightest tincture of malignity."[4] It were strange, indeed, if he should offend his few beloved friends, and spoil their good fellowship with any irritating stings of *malignity*. This kind of venom, which he possessed in good store, he reserved for the Christian religion, and its ministers: And how could a sincere friend of virtue be so implacably severe upon Christianity? Does it not carry virtue to its summit of perfection? Are not many of our clergy as virtuous? Are they not, according to their ability, at least as liberal in charity as any the most generous of our infidels? And though multitudes professing Christianity are dissolute and worthless, because they consider not its nature and importance, are there not many Christians of every rank who excel in virtue, and are virtuous from a nobler principle than infidels can be—from love, influenced by the amiable perfections of the Deity, and these shining in the height of their glory in Jesus Christ? Some, indeed, are generous from constitutional humanity; and as we Christians know, upon the most satisfactory evidence, that the gospel only is powerful to form the heart of man to true divine virtue, we may be allowed, consistently with charity, to suppose, yea, positively to assert, that the virtues of our infidel sophists are very lame and contracted; that the few of them which they seem to respect are tinged with the enormous pride and vanity which speak loftily in all their ingenious labours, especially in their painful lucubrations pointed at the overthrow of revelation; for effecting which laudable purpose, they, with great parade, bring up the auxiliary engine of zeal for virtue, with a superficial shew of it in life. Let their virtues be examined with severe scrutiny, and shall they not "be found wanting"[5]; blazing high in words, but glimmering faintly in life? Are they not so far from perfection, that they are miserably destitute of that singleness which is essential to genuine virtue? In vain do infidel philosophers pretend that they are the only

4. See p. 51 in this volume.
5. See Daniel 5:27.

students of human nature; that, from their scientific theories, the world is to learn virtue. Indeed, none seem to mistake it more than they do: from what principle, and for what reason, we are not ignorant. One reason is, that, being self-confident, they disdain consulting the Bible, in which the truest account of virtue lies obvious before all, and which, I may say, is the only true history of human nature in the world.

Can any thing be more frivolous, more childish, more indecently wanton and presumptuous in a dying man, perceiving himself on the verge of time, than Mr H–'s sportful dialogue with *Charon*?—Is this nature? Is it sober reason?—To take leave of this world, of its various alluring comforts, an affluent fortune, a distinguished reputation, the agreeable society of friends, lively health and good chear, inchanting diversions and amusements;—to bid an eternal farewel to all these delights of the sons of men, without the prospect of better things, or of their equivalent in another state, but darkling to plunge into a dreary abyss, "a land of darkness, as darkness itself,"[6] under absolute uncertainty what his lot may be—whether a miserable eternal existence in separation from the body, or annihilation. To depart thus sceptical with a perfectly easy mind, without sad regret, without a wishful look "after what his soul delighted in,"[7] now flying from his sight! It cannot be—it contradicts the essential principles of nature. And was he really chearful without hope? Let him believe it who can! Those who allow themselves to understand human nature as it really is, cannot help suspecting that all this specious tranquillity must have been affected. True, indeed, the scripture says of some, "whom pride compasseth about as a chain, that there are no bands in their death"; that, being "given up to a reprobate (unfeeling) mind, they live and die in a profound peace," singing a *requiem*, "peace and safety, when destruction is near."[8]

Mr H–'s singular composure in the near view of death, the doctor stiles *magnanimity*.[9] What—to brave and jest with death!—death, so terrible to nature! with pertinacious contempt of its consequences!—Do you call this *magnanimity*? Is it not better named *foolhardiness*?—Consult nature, Dr S–h; consult common sense, and speak out what it dictates. Why should

6. See Job 10:22.
7. See Isaiah 66:3.
8. See Psalms 73:4–6; Romans 1:28; and 1 Thessalonians 5:3.
9. See pp. 46 and 48 in this volume.

you be emulous of sharing in the reputation of a philosophy which commits an outrage at once against the sacred oracles, and the common feelings of humanity.

We are told that Mr H– was quite resigned.[10] Resigned! to what? Not to the will of God. Of his name and will we hear not a word "in the course of his chearful conversation." He was resigned, it may be said, to the constitution of things—to the order of nature. An order of nature, exclusive of the Author of nature, are words without meaning. With such worldly obscure wisdom, vain men, who affect to be wiser than scripture, presume to put a blind upon the world; "who, professing themselves to be wise, are become fools; vain in their imaginations, and their foolish hearts hardened."[11]

How miserable the comforter, who could minister no other consolation to his dying friend, than "that he was to leave his friends in great prosperity!"[12] Alas! to leave his abundant wealth to others, and nothing left to himself in its place, but the mortifying prospect of death and worms soon to devour him! And is the man, the wise man now comforted? A fine flight this of disinterested benevolence! It sounds pompously in speculation; but did it ever exist in any man's mind? Never: nor in Dr S–th's, nor in mine, nor in the almost perfect Mr H–'s. When this pitiful *cordial* is presented, he still needed the *balsam* of *Lucian*'s droll tale about *Charon* and his boat to assuage, or rather to divert, the wounding thought of parting with the delicacies of the world, without the hope of better, or of as good in their place.

Upon the supposition Mr H– had no wealth to leave, to what resource shall he now turn for comfort? What remains to bear up his heart? "All refuge fails."[13] The poor man must be quite inconsolable!—O how much easier and happier is royal *David* in his exit! What other sort of dignity does he exhibit in dying? who, notwithstanding the unfavourable aspect of his family, could joyfully say, "Although my house be not so with

10. See p. 46 in this volume.

11. See Romans 1:21–22.

12. See p. 47 in this volume.

13. There are many possible references here, if indeed a single reference was intended. Perhaps the most likely is John Bunyan, "Come, and Welcome, to Jesus Christ; or, A Plain and Profitable Discourse on John vi.37," in *The Works of that Eminent Servant of Christ, Mr John Bunyan*, fourth edition, vol. 3 (Edinburgh: Sands, Murray, and Cochran, 1769), 18.

God, yet he hath made with me an everlasting covenant, &c."[14]—Compare together a sceptical philosopher and a scripture saint in dying, and see the abject meanness into which the one sinks—the grandeur, in hope of everlasting glory, to which the other rises.—*Jacob*, in blessing and taking leave of the tribes on his death-bed, is divinely composed with the hope of "God's salvation."[15]—*David* launches forth fearless into the dark vale, assuredly believing that God would be his guide to glory.[16]—How *truly magnanimous* is *Paul* in facing death, greatly triumphing in hope of a never-fading crown of righteousness?[17] Where now is the wise man? "Where the philosophic disputer of this world,"[18] who denies revelation and immortality? Can he compare, for true greatness, with the meanest Christian *dying in faith*? O heaven! what a dark, melancholy scene must this world be? how joyless the short life of man in it, had he not God to trust in, no immortal life to hope for, no principle to be guided and supported by, but "let us eat and drink, for to-morrow we die."[19]

Suppose the proofs of revelation were doubtful, and not so satisfactory as they are, is it not more for the good of the world, more for the honour, for the comfort, and happiness of mankind, to admit, than to question its truth? The effects of true faith in scripture dignify and exalt human nature in life and in death. What so powerful to influence the practice of virtue, to support under the evils of life, and in the last conflict with death, as are the comforts of the gospel? Philosophers will tell us, that to the practice of virtue, another motive is necessary than the attraction of its own beauty. And where is its beauty displayed to such perfection as in scripture? But, besides the beauty of virtue, such degenerate creatures as we are, and in such a tempting world as this, do need further subsidiary motives of divine authority, and the lively hope of a happy immortality, to hold us to its practice with persevering fortitude.—In the death of a true Christian, divinely submissive to the will of God, and amid the pains of dissolving nature, exulting in the hope of eternal glory, you have an exalted view of human nature; whereas dark, hopeless infidelity degrades man into the

14. See 2 Samuel 23:5.
15. See Genesis 49:18.
16. See Psalms 23:4.
17. See 2 Timothy 4:8.
18. See 1 Corinthians 1:20.
19. See 1 Corinthians 15:32.

"likeness of a beast that perisheth."[20] When I reflect upon that grave saying of Jesus, "If ye believe not that I am He, ye shall die in your sins,"[21] I cannot but lament the death of an Infidel.

Good God! to what a pitch of incredulity and callousness do curious men, with fruitless labour, from a vain affectation of singularity, work themselves? What scripture says, Isa. xlvii.10. applies properly to such men; "Their wisdom and their knowledge hath perverted them, and they say in their hearts (and in words too), we are, and none else besides us."—But, however much they value themselves upon their ingenious subtleties, they shall not by them prevail, they shall not succeed in their malevolent designs against revelation; nor shall they, by their impotent attempts to overthrow it, establish what they most affect, a name of immortal renown. They are sure to be vexed with a disappointment of their hope with respect to both. Their proselytes shall be only among the vain and vicious, who, without the help of false philosophy, are of themselves disposed to get free of the restraints of religion, and for liberty to live at large, form their notion of virtue, after their own hearts. Their elaborate theories, by which they gain the temporary fame of genius exerted, are of such manifestly evil tendency, so inimical to Christianity, and to men's best interests, that they can never go down with the wise and virtuous, but must be abjured by them; and shall therefore, it is hoped, meet with deserved contempt and neglect from our princes, our nobles, our judges, from our learned gentlemen of every order, and from all people who revere God and love mankind.

I am, SIR,

Yours, &c.

E. M.

*B–r–h* , *April* 17.

20. See Psalms 49:12, 20.
21. See John 8:24.

# Observations Relative to the Late David Hume, Esq.

"Idem."

*Lord, how are they increased that trouble me! Many are they that rise up against me; many there be which say of my soul, There is no help for him in God. Selah.*

PSALM iii.[1]

SIR,

When a great man comes to town, we have it in the papers next day: though there should be nothing of the marvellous in the manner of his arrival, yet it is a satisfaction to know it; but when a man of eminence is sent to hell, there are such unavoidable delays, owing to the distance—the badness of the roads, and other circumstances, that we cannot have the pleasure of hearing such great news till many months after his decease.

It was, I think, in March or April, 1773, that the late celebrated earl of Ch–f–d died, and it was not till March 1775 that his damnation was notified in your Magazine by an elegant writer who subscribes himself *Eusebius*.[2] It is, therefore, less surprising that we have not had an earlier account of the fate of the late David Hume, Esq; who died in August last, than that in your Magazine, P. 141. communicated by a gentle-

1. See Psalms 3:1–2.

2. Philip Dormer Stanhope, 4th Earl of Chesterfield (1694–1773), was an English politician, writer, and wit who was notorious for flouting the social conventions of the British aristocracy. He died on 24 March 1773. For the letter by "Eusebius," see "REFLECTIONS *occasioned by reading the* ACCOUNT *of the Death of Lord* CH----F--D. *To the* PUBLISHER *of the* WEEKLY MAGAZINE," in *The Weekly Magazine, or Edinburgh Amusement*, vol. 28 (30 March 1775), 3–6.

man who signs the initials E. M.[3] Both Eusebius and Mr E. M. decline disclosing the sources of their intelligence, though every man must be sensible they would not have hazarded such assertions without something more convincing than mere speculation to warrant them. They chuse rather to treat that affair as a point of doctrine, than as an article of intelligence, and produce proofs rather than authorities; indeed, they bring such damning proof, that there is little occasion for any thing else to convince the greatest admirers of these eminent men of their deplorable condition. Thus the doctrine of these men's perdition resembles, in some measure, those great truths which men could never have found out of themselves, but being imparted by revelation, have afterwards been made out by reason.

With regard to Mr Hume, it is a consummation devoutly to be wished for by every good Scotsman.[4] This man, without having the fear of poverty before his eyes, from which our whole nation are scampering away to the tune of *Devil take the hindmost*, trifled away the best part of his life in improving his mind, and had the effrontery to produce such works as no other Scotsman was ever capable of, and to display such candour, moderation, impartiality, penetration, and taste, as was never heard, or seen, or conceived, in this country before; and we hope, for the preservation of that national character which we have enjoyed ever since Fergus I.[5] will never be imitated while sun and moon endure. It is chiefly to his preposterous exertions that we owe a literary reputation, for which we had no occasion, which we have no prospect of ever being able to support, and which will soon bring us into double disgrace with the nations around us, by raising expectations that we can never answer. Should his lukewarm sceptical humour, which has already chilled the native fire of so many of our youth, continue to spread its baleful influence, we shall soon be deprived of that characteristical fervour, which formerly impelled us to so many surprising undertakings. The only thing that can alleviate the evils that are come upon us through his means, is that good news which your correspondent's letter affords us, which may be very useful in deterring others from the like attempts for many years to come: yet many are so hardened, that they

3. See pp. 75–80 in this volume.
4. See William Shakespeare, *Hamlet*, Act 3, scene 1.
5. Fergus I is the mythical first king of Scotland who allegedly ruled in the fourth century B.C.

raise objections to the solid arguments upon which this salutary doctrine of Hume's perdition is grounded, nay, even some professed Christians have ventured to cavil against it.

I shall repeat some of those things I have heard advanced against your correspondent's reasoning, without attempting to answer them, though that would be no hard task, because the honour properly belongs to him of settling, beyond dispute, that great and important truth in which we all have need to be well established, in such trying and shaking times.

1. Some take upon them to deny that Mr Hume acted the fool at his end;[6] for they say that his conversation and behaviour was so much in the usual strain,[7] that this argument would prove too much, as even his enemies do not pretend that he lived like a fool.

2. They likewise deny that he died indecently humorous[8]; for they alledge that there is nothing in the humorous part of Mr Hume's conversation, recited by Dr Smith, but what is decent enough, and that conversation happened more than a fortnight before his death. They do not presume, however, to deny, that if a man should happen to laugh upon any occasion, and be so ill advised as to die within twenty-fours after, it might go hard with him.

3. They deny that he died *seemingly easy*,[9] for they affirm that he died easy in truth and reality.[10]

5. That he died without hope,[11] they endeavour to disprove by the testimony of his physician, who writes that he died in such a happy composure of mind, that nothing could exceed it.[12]

6. That he was perfectly impious, and a downright Atheist,[13] they say is a charge that should never be brought against any man without bringing some reasons to support it. When I heard them talk at this rate, I begged them to hold their peace, for they only exposed their own ignorance. Ever since the world began, all such men as Hume have been reckoned Atheists and impious wretches, and sometimes treated as such, and nobody

6. See p. 75 in this volume.
7. See p. 46 in this volume.
8. See p. 75 in this volume.
9. See p. 75 in this volume.
10. There is no fourth point in the list as printed.
11. See p. 75 in this volume.
12. See p. 50 in this volume.
13. See p. 75 in this volume.

was ever so foolish as to ask what was the reason of it. That they are such, is one of those primary truths which strike the mind at once, and are incapable of being deduced by reasoning from any of the principles of human knowledge. It is a truth, of which the most illiterate clowns[14] are fully convinced, merely by its own evidence, without the smallest aid of reasoning: the common sense of mankind teaches it.

7. That he rested on his virtue[15] they do not intirely deny, but that he laid more weight on it than it was able to support, requires to be proved. They assert boldly, that he had more modesty than he had occasion for.

8. That his virtues were tinged with enormous pride and vanity,[16] is a charge, they say, that destroys itself, while the meaning of these words remains the same as at present.

9. That he disdained consulting the Bible,[17] is what they are surprised to hear, when they consider how many strokes in his works discover greater intimacy with that book, than falls to the share of some of those who are paid for studying it.

10. They alledge further, that he did not jest with death, nor brave it,[18] but waited its approach with great composure; and though he had jested with death, he was not much to blame, as it appears from the account of his lingering illness, that death had long jested with him.

11. That he outraged the sacred oracles, and the common feelings of humanity,[19] they aver, is as difficult to be proved, as all the other charges brought against them. If the scripture represents the wicked as tortured with remorse at the approach of death, he did nothing to prevent the fulfilling of the scripture; as he had not been a wicked man, it was none of his business to die with remorse. His last letter to Dr Smith shows that he still retained some feelings of humanity, and some grains of politeness.

12. That he left nothing to himself,[20] they say, is not strictly true, for he still retained something of a good conscience, and hopes of a better state,

14. The word "clown" had a very different meaning in the eighteenth century than it has today; Samuel Johnson's dictionary defines the term as "a rustick; a country fellow; a churl" or "a coarse ill-bred man." Johnson, "Clown," in *A Dictionary of the English Language*.

15. See p. 76 in this volume.

16. See p. 76 in this volume.

17. See p. 77 in this volume.

18. See p. 77 in this volume.

19. See p. 78 in this volume.

20. See p. 78 in this volume.

and a reputation for learning and genius so peculiarly his own, that none of his contemporaries can have any share in it. They add further, with great assurance, that this charge would have been more heavily urged, if it had been thus worded, "He left nothing to Mr E. M."

Such are the pitiful cavils with which they endeavour to impugn a doctrine of the greatest importance to the consolation and upbuilding of very many respectable and serious people. No doubt, Mr E. M. your correspondent, will soon answer them so effectually, as for ever to stop the mouths of these vain babblers.

In the mean time, there are some of his arguments that, with all their malice, they have not been able to shake. It is undeniable, that God was not in any of his words, from which Mr E. M. rightly infers, that he was not resigned to the will of God.[21] This whole argument is founded upon this great truth, that God is not named in those parts of Mr Hume's conversation recited in Dr Smith's letter. Let any intelligent person carefully examine that letter, laying his finger upon every line where Mr Hume is introduced speaking (that he may be sure not to miss one of them), and if he there find the word GOD, Mr E. M. and I are willing to allow this argument to have no weight or force; nay, if he examine the whole letter in the same manner, he will be convinced, that Dr Smith and Dr Black are as hardened and regardless of God as Mr Hume.—Such is the force of bad example!

Another thing that must for ever ascertain Mr Hume's condemnation is, that he was venomous to the clergy. Other profligate persons have treated these holy men injuriously, and brought false accusations against them, which gave them no small trouble to clear themselves from; but Mr Hume has carried his malignity so far, that he has said things against them which they will never be able to answer. To lay things to men's charge that are too true to be denied, is being venomous to the highest degree.

These quibbling defenders of Mr Hume have not been able to justify his reading such profane authors as Lucian within a month of his death; it is a thing that will admit of no palliation. Indeed, I tremble when I consider the desperate wickedness of our professors and schoolmasters, who are so hardened, that I have seen some of them stand with an erect countenance, in the midst of a large room, prelecting to a croud of scholars from such profane authors as Anacreon, Xenophon, Terence, and Horace, whilst, in

21. See p. 78 in this volume.

the mean time, they did not know but that they were standing on the brink of eternity, and, in the twinkling of an eye, the house might tumble about their ears and crush them to atoms.

How well this poor man deserved that fate, which it so evidently appears he has found, the serious reader will easily perceive if he considers the following particulars:

Though he knew he was born to a small fortune, and that knowledge and prudence are of much more value than riches, power, or pleasure, yet he was seized early with a passion for literature, which became the ruling passion of his life.[22]

Though he knew that God has fixed no limits to human industry, but has given us the faculty of reason to exert and improve, to the utmost, in every useful and innocent inquiry, yet he ventured to think for himself, and, what is more, to differ in opinion, not only from his predecessors, but even from his cotemporaries, and some of them younger than himself.

Though he knew that he was liable, like most other men, to fall into mistakes, and entertain false opinions, yet he insulted the common sense of mankind to such a degree, that he scarce ever advanced any thing in his writings without attempting to prove it.

So little regard had he for truth, that neglecting and despising all those methods which have been invented for its defence, and established as the laws of disputation among all civilized nations, he neither impeached the morals, abused the persons, vilified the understandings, insulted the misfortunes, nor put malicious constructions on the words and actions of those who did not immediately adopt all his new-fangled notions, but left his reasonings to stand or fall by their own merit.

Though he knew that impartiality is one of the first duties of an historian, and that the bitterness which gives such relish and poignancy to modern history is but ill calculated to improve posterity, yet he was so besotted as to neglect attaching himself to that party which was in a capacity to reward his labours,[23] and, as if he had not been a Scotsman, but only a citizen of the world, he exposed, with great coolness, the excesses of those who contended for liberty, as well as for those who defended the prerogative.

Though he knew that death was appointed for all men, and that melancholy or anxiety could be of no avail in averting the stroke, yet he waited for it with cheerfulness and intrepidity.

---

22. See p. 36 in this volume.
23. See pp. 40–41 in this volume.

And to crown all, and fill up the cup of his iniquities, though he knew that a time of sickness and languishing is improper for serious studies, yet in his last illness he amused himself with books of entertainment, and talked facetiously of his own death in Lucian's manner on the 8th of August 1776, although it was decreed that he was to depart this life on the 25th of the same month, and though he was unapprised of that decree.

What a different reputation would this man have left, had he followed a quite contrary course! How much more would he have been regreted by your ingenious correspondent, and that numerous and respectable part of the nation who think like him.

Had he spent the prime of his life in the diligent use of all feasible means of acquiring riches, without reckoning any other object deserving of his attention; had he prudently regarded human affairs no farther than to make them contribute as much as possible to the advancement of his fortune; had he left all consideration of divine things to those who are appointed by law to watch over them; or, if he must needs dabble in philosophy and reasoning, had he confined himself to the beaten track, and employed his talents in vilifying every one who ventured to depart from it one inch either to the right hand or to the left; had he abstained from corrupting the age with a dangerous scepticism, but rather asserted the most unintelligible propositions with a manly boldness, and disdained the mean artifices of reasoning and investigation, so much esteemed by the disputers of this world; had he, on the approach of death, shown that becoming contrition and tenderness of spirit which makes the last period of life so edifying to spectators; had he expressed a sincere regret for every profane and undutiful expression that he had ever in his life thrown out against the ministers of the gospel, charging them with any of the imperfections of human nature; had he spent his last days in committing to memory the choicest compositions of his namesake, the royal Psalmist, to assist him, in behaving godly, by retailing them upon his death-bed; had he conducted himself thus through life, and in death, he would have left a memory dear and venerable to the far greater part of his countrymen, and his friends would not have been shocked with the news of his damnation in public prints.

Yours, &c.

IDEM.

*April* 26.

# Bibliography


Aristotle. *Nicomachean Ethics*, translated by Robert C. Bartlett and Susan D. Collins. Chicago: University of Chicago Press, 2011.

Baier, Annette C. "Hume's Deathbed Reading: A Tale of Three Letters." In *Death and Character: Further Reflections on Hume*. Cambridge, MA: Harvard University Press, 2008.

———. *The Pursuits of Philosophy: An Introduction to the Life and Thought of David Hume*. Cambridge, MA: Harvard University Press, 2011.

Ballestrem, Karl Graf. "David Hume und Adam Smith: Zur philosophischen Dimension einer Freundschaft." In *Adam Smith als Moralphilosoph*, edited by Christel Fricke and Hans-Peter Schütt. Berlin: Walter de Gruyter, 2005.

Baumstark, Maurice. "The End of Empire and the Death of Religion: A Reconsideration of Hume's Later Political Thought." In *Philosophy and Religion in Enlightenment Britain*, edited by Ruth Savage. Oxford: Oxford University Press, 2012.

Beattie, James. *An Essay on the Immutability of Truth; In Opposition to Sophistry and Scepticism*. Edinburgh: A. Kincaid and J. Bell, 1770.

Boswell, James. *Boswell in Extremes, 1776–1778*, edited by Charles McC. Weis and Frederick A. Pottle. New York: McGraw-Hill, 1970.

———. *Boswell: Laird of Auchinleck, 1778–1782*, edited by Joseph W. Reed and Frederick A. Pottle. New York: McGraw Hill, 1977.

———. *Journal of a Tour to the Hebrides with Samuel Johnson, LL.D.*, edited by Frederick A. Pottle and Charles H. Bennett. New York: McGraw-Hill, [1785] 1961.

———. *The Life of Samuel Johnson*, edited by David Womersley. New York: Penguin, [1791] 2008.

Brown, Iain Gordon. "Introduction: 'Embalming a Philosopher' – The Writing, Reception, and Resonance of David Hume's 'My Own Life.'" In *David Hume: My Own Life*, edited by Iain Gordon Brown. Edinburgh: Royal Society of Edinburgh, 2014.

Bunyan, John. "Come, and Welcome, to Jesus Christ; or, A Plain and Profitable Discourse on John vi.37." In *The Works of that Eminent Servant of Christ, Mr John Bunyan*, fourth edition, volume 3. Edinburgh: Sands, Murray, and Cochran, 1769.

Campbell, T. D., and Ian Ross. "The Theory and Practice of the Wise and Virtuous Man: Reflections on Adam Smith's Response to Hume's Deathbed Wish." *Studies in Eighteenth-Century Culture* 11 (1982): 65–75.

Cicero. *De Senectute*. In *On Old Age, On Friendship, On Divination*, translated by W. A. Falconer. Cambridge, MA: Harvard University Press, 1923.

Corsa, Andrew. "Modern Greatness of Soul in Hume and Smith." *Ergo* 2, no. 2 (2015): 27–58.

Crawford, Thomas, editor. *The Correspondence of James Boswell and William Johnson Temple, 1756–1795, Volume 1: 1756–1777*. New Haven: Yale University Press, 1997.

Fieser, James, editor. *Early Responses to Hume*, second edition. Ten volumes. Bristol, UK: Thoemmes Continuum, 2005.

Flanders, Chad. "Hume's Death and Smith's Philosophy." In *New Essays on Adam Smith's Moral Philosophy*, edited by Wade L. Robison and David B. Suits. Rochester, NY: Rochester Institute of Technology Press, 2012.

Fleischacker, Samuel. "Smith's Ambiguities: A Response to Emma Rothschild's *Economic Sentiments*." *Adam Smith Review* 1 (2004): 141–49.

Gaskin, J. C. A. "Hume on Religion." In *The Cambridge Companion to Hume*, second edition, edited by David Fate Norton and Jacqueline Taylor. Cambridge: Cambridge University Press, 2009.

Greig, J. Y. T. *David Hume*. New York: Garland, [1931] 1983.

Haldane, Alexander. *Memoirs of the Lives of Robert Haldane of Airthrey, and of His Brother, James Alexander Haldane*. London: Hamilton, Adams, and Co., 1852.

Hanley, Ryan Patrick. "Skepticism and Imagination: Smith's Response to Hume's *Dialogues*." In *New Essays on Adam Smith's Moral Philosophy*, edited by Wade L. Robison and David B. Suits. Rochester, NY: Rochester Institute of Technology Press, 2012.

Hill, G. Birkbeck, editor. *Letters of David Hume to William Strahan*. Oxford: Clarendon, 1888.

Hume, David. *An Enquiry Concerning Human Understanding*, edited by Tom L. Beauchamp. Oxford: Clarendon, [1748] 2000.

———. *An Enquiry Concerning the Principles of Morals*, edited by Tom L. Beauchamp. Oxford: Clarendon, [1751] 1998.

———. *A Treatise of Human Nature*, edited by David Fate Norton and Mary J. Norton. Oxford: Clarendon, [1739–40] 2007.

Ikeda, Sadao. *David Hume and the Eighteenth Century British Thought: An Annotated Catalogue*. Tokyo: Chuo University Library, 1986.

Johnson, Samuel. *A Dictionary of the English Language*, volume 1. London: W. Strahan, 1755.

Keble, John, editor. *The Works of That Learned and Judicious Divine Mr. Richard Hooker*, seventh edition. Oxford: Clarendon, 1888.

Kennedy, Gavin. *Adam Smith's Lost Legacy*. New York: Palgrave Macmillan, 2005.

Long, Brendan. "Adam Smith's Theism." In *The Elgar Companion to Adam Smith*, edited by Jeffrey T. Young. Cheltenham, UK: Edward Elgar, 2009.

Lowrie, John M. *The Life of David*. Philadelphia: Presbyterian Board of Publication, 1869.

Mackenzie, Henry. *An Account of the Life and Writings of John Home, Esq.* Edinburgh: Archibald Constable and Co., 1822.

Minowitz, Peter. *Profits, Priests, and Princes: Adam Smith's Emancipation of Economics from Politics and Religion*. Stanford: Stanford University Press, 1993.

Mossner, Ernest Campbell. *The Life of David Hume*, second edition. Oxford: Clarendon, 1980.

———. "Philosophy and Biography: The Case of David Hume." *Philosophical Review* 59, no. 2 (April 1950): 184–201.

Oslington, Paul, editor. *Adam Smith as Theologian*. New York: Routledge, 2011.

Panofsky, Erwin. "Et in Arcadia Ego." In *Philosophy & History: Essays Presented to Ernst Cassirer*, edited by Raymond Klibansky and H. J. Paton. Oxford: Clarendon, 1936.

Phillipson, Nicholas. *Adam Smith: An Enlightened Life*. New Haven: Yale University Press, 2010.

Plato. *Phaedo*. In *The Collected Dialogues of Plato*, edited by Edith Hamilton and Huntington Cairns. Princeton: Princeton University Press, 1961.

Pope, Alexander. *The Major Works*, edited by Pat Rogers. Oxford: Oxford University Press, 2006.

Pratt, Samuel Jackson. *An Apology for the Life and Writings of David Hume, Esq.: With a Parallel Between Him and the Late Lord Chesterfield: To Which Is Added an Address to One of the People Called Christians, By Way of Reply to His Letter to Adam Smith*. London: Fielding and Walker, 1777.

———. *Supplement to the Life of David Hume, Esq., Containing Genuine Anecdotes, and a Circumstantial Account of His Death and Funeral.* London: J. Bew, 1777.

Rae, John. *Life of Adam Smith.* New York: Augustus M. Kelley, [1895] 1965.

Ramsay of Ochtertyre, John. *Scotland and Scotsmen in the Eighteenth Century*, edited by Alexander Allardyce, volume 1. Edinburgh: William Blackwood, 1888.

Rasmussen, Dennis C. *The Infidel and the Professor: David Hume, Adam Smith, and the Friendship That Shaped Modern Thought.* Princeton: Princeton University Press, 2017.

Ross, Ian Simpson. *The Life of Adam Smith*, second edition. Oxford: Oxford University Press, 2010.

Rothschild, Emma. "Dignity or Meanness." *Adam Smith Review* 1 (2004): 150–64.

———. *Economic Sentiments: Adam Smith, Condorcet, and the Enlightenment.* Cambridge, MA: Harvard University Press, 2001.

Schliesser, Eric. "Obituary of a Vain Philosopher: Adam Smith's Reflections on Hume's Life." *Hume Studies* 29, no. 2 (November 2003): 327–62.

Smith, Adam. *An Inquiry into the Nature and Causes of the Wealth of Nations*, edited by R. H. Campbell, A. S. Skinner, and W. B. Todd. Indianapolis: Liberty Fund [1776], 1981.

———. *Lectures on Rhetoric and Belles Lettres*, edited by J. C. Bryce. Indianapolis: Liberty Fund, [1762–63] 1985.

———. *The Theory of Moral Sentiments*, edited by D. D. Raphael and A. L. Macfie. Indianapolis: Liberty Fund, [1759–90] 1982.

Stewart, Dugald. *Account of the Life and Writings of Adam Smith, LL.D.*, edited by I. S. Ross. In Adam Smith, *Essays on Philosophical Subjects*. Indianapolis: Liberty Fund, [1794] 1980.

Stewart, M. A. "The Dating of Hume's Manuscripts." In *The Scottish Enlightenment: Essays in Reinterpretation*, edited by Paul Wood. Rochester, NY: University of Rochester Press, 2000.

Streminger, Gerhard. "David Hume and John Home: Two New Letters." *Hume Studies* 10, no. 1 (April 1984): 81–83.

Thomson, John. *An Account of the Life, Lectures, and Writings of William Cullen, M. D.*, volume 1. Edinburgh: William Blackwood, 1832.

Todd, William B. "David Hume: A Preliminary Bibliography." In *Hume and the Enlightenment: Essays Presented to Ernest Campbell Mossner*, edited by William B. Todd. Edinburgh: Edinburgh University Press, 1974.

Virgil. *The Aeneid*, translated by Robert Fagles. New York: Penguin, 2006.

Voltaire. "A Letter from the Author to Mr. S. Gravesand, Professor of Mathematics." In *The Works of M. de Voltaire*, translated by Tobias Smollett, volume 18. London: J. Newbery et al., 1762.

Walker, Ralph S., editor. *The Correspondence of James Boswell and John Johnston of Grange*. New York: McGraw-Hill, 1966.

Wesley, John. "On the Deceitfulness of the Human Heart." In *The Works of the Rev. John Wesley, A. M.*, third edition, volume 7. London: John Mason, [1790] 1829.

Wilkinson, J. "The Last Illness of David Hume." *Proceedings of the Royal College of Physicians of Edinburgh* 18, no. 1 (January 1988): 72–79.

# Index

# About the Author

**Dennis C. Rasmussen** is Professor of Political Science at Tufts University. His research interests center on the Enlightenment and on the virtues and shortcomings of liberal democracy and market capitalism. He is the author of *The Infidel and the Professor: David Hume, Adam Smith, and the Friendship That Shaped Modern Thought* (Princeton University Press, 2017), *The Pragmatic Enlightenment: Recovering the Liberalism of Hume, Smith, Montesquieu, and Voltaire* (Cambridge University Press, 2014), and *The Problems and Promise of Commercial Society: Adam Smith's Response to Rousseau* (Penn State University Press, 2008).